Richard Beale 07/24
May 1978

Revolutionary Tracts

By
John Joachim Zubly

1. *The Stamp Act Repealed.* Originally published in 1766.

2. *An Humble Enquiry into the Nature of the Dependency of the American Colonies upon the Parliament of Great-Britain and the Right of Parliament to Lay Taxes on the Said Colonies.* Originally published in 1769.

3. *The Law of Liberty.* Originally published in 1775.

The Reprint Company
Spartanburg, South Carolina

This Volume Was Reproduced
From Original Editions
In The
University of Georgia Libraries
Athens, Georgia

The Reprint Company
Post Office Box 5401
Spartanburg, South Carolina 29301

Reprinted: 1972
ISBN 0-87152-088-5
Library of Congress Catalog Card Number: 75-187393

Manufactured in the United States of America on long-life paper.

Publisher's Note

With the publication of this volume, The Reprint Company brings together three very rare pieces of source material on Georgia and the American Revolution by Reverend John Joachim Zubly, a pre-Revolutionary activist in Georgia and a member of the Second Continental Congress.

One of the sermons reprinted—"The Stamp Act Repealed" —was first published in 1766 and has been described as possibly the rarest bit of printed Georgia material on the American Revolution. The other sermon, "The Law of Liberty," was delivered at the opening of the Georgia Provincial Congress in 1775.

The third item included is a pamphlet, published first in 1769, which examines the ". . . Dependency of the American Colonies upon the Parliament of Great-Britain and the Right of Parliament to Lay Taxes on the Said Colonies."

The introduction, by Dr. Kenneth Coleman of the University of Georgia, deals more with Zubly and his place in Georgia than with his actual writings. Zubly's ideas can be taken from the sermons and pamphlet reprinted.

# # #

In the reproduction of centuries-old material such as this, problems develop at times which, it is hoped, will not interfere with the reader's pleasure at having it available once again.

One of the constant problems is locating original copies clean and clear enough to photograph. This proved to be a major problem in the publication of this reprint edition.

The originals of the Zubly sermons and pamphlet reprinted here are owned by the University of Georgia in Athens. Because of the rarity and condition of the items involved, the material was placed on microfilm and this reprint was produced from that.

170487

One of the technical problems in the process of reproduction is to provide equal density for all pages and this is not always possible when it does not exist in the original copy. Consequently, the reader will notice some unevenness in the printing from page to page and some of the words may appear blurred.

It is hoped that these discrepancies in this reprint edition will appear slight to the reader. The publisher believes that making the material available again in this form outweighs the disadvantage of having it available only in the vault of a rare book collection.

The Reprint Company

Introduction

The Reverend John Joachim Zubly (August 27, 1724–July 23, 1781) was born in St. Gall, one of the German cantons in Switzerland, and educated in the gymnasium there. In 1743 the German and Swiss Calvinists in the new American colony of Georgia requested that Zubly be sent to Georgia as their minister. Two years later he arrived and soon became an assistant to the Savannah Anglican minister, the Reverend Bartholomew Zouberbuhler, also a German Swiss. Zubly's special duty was to preach to the German and French settlers. Apparently Zubly and Zouberbuhler did not get along well, so after some two years Zubly moved to South Carolina, where his father already lived. He preached in South Carolina and quite probably in Georgia on occasional visits. In 1760 Zubly returned to Savannah as minister of the Independent Meeting House, a Presbyterian congregation.

Zubly soon became a leading clergyman and citizen in Georgia. He preached to Calvinists and Lutherans in French, in German, or in English, as the congregation desired. He acquired land and slaves and did quite well economically. His popularity with the people was shown through election to such offices as that of clerk in the local parish government in Savannah. Zubly corresponded with Ezra Stiles and other leading Puritan clergymen. He became well enough known to be awarded a M.A. in 1770 and a D.D. in 1774 by the College of New Jersey (Princeton), the leading Presbyterian college in America.

Zubly soon made himself the leading defender of the rights of religious dissenters in Georgia, always insisting that these rights be upheld by the government. He carried on a protracted and sometimes intense argument with the Reverend Samuel Frink, a somewhat legalistic and intolerant Anglican rector in Savannah. The two ministers argued about such things as the rector's rights to clergyman's fees when a dissenter performed the actual religious service. Zubly fought Frink with partial success on the rights of dissenters to be buried in the public burial ground in Savannah and the right of Jews to have a burial ground granted for their use. Zubly's extensive reading in English history and law made him an able antagonist. He enjoyed a good argument and fought for what he believed to be right, but he was also tedious and doubtless difficult to work with.

It is as a participant in the pre-revolutionary activities in Georgia that Zubly is best remembered. From the Stamp Act of 1765 to his election to the Second Continental Congress in 1775, Zubly's activities established him as a Whig who would do all in his power to secure for Americans the rights of Englishmen under the British constitution. Zubly's contribution to the developing political rhetoric of the decade was in his ideas on the British constitution—not new nor radical concepts, but concepts similar to those held and argued for by many other Americans. First and foremost among these concepts was the belief that the constitution created a government of law which guaranteed liberty for the subject. Zubly used the historical argument to prove that the colonies had been controlled by the crown rather than by Parliament, and should continue to be so controlled. He insisted that Parliament had no right to tax colonials because Englishmen could only be taxed by their representatives, and colonials were not represented in the Parliament at Westminster. Therefore Zubly argued that by law, by constitutional right, and by historical precedent Parliament could not tax the colonials. And when the Declaratory Act, passed by Parliament with the repeal of the Stamp Act in 1766, maintained Parliament's right to bind the colonies "in all cases whatsoever," Zubly strenuously objected.

Like most Americans, Zubly saw the British constitution as a body of fixed principles, not something which Parliament could change at will. Acts of Parliament disagreeing with these principles were tyranny and should not be allowed to stand. The popularity of Zubly's sermons and writings was attested to when he was elected a member of the Georgia Provincial

Congress in 1775 and asked to preach a special sermon, "The Law of Liberty," at the opening of the Congress. He became a member of the Congress committees which prepared an address to Royal Governor Sir James Wright, a petition to the king, a letter to the Continental Congress, and a statement to the people of Georgia. Finally the Congress elected Zubly as one of the five delegates to represent Georgia in the Continental Congress then meeting in Philadelphia. Zubly entered into the work of that body after his arrival early in September and remained until the drift towards independence became stronger. He left Philadelphia in mid-November and returned to Savannah to discover that his opposition to independence had ended much of his previous popularity.

In July of 1776 Zubly was arrested by the newly created state government since he was considered a danger to public safety, but he was soon released. In September of 1777 people of doubtful loyalty were required to take an oath of allegiance to Georgia and to the United States or be banished and have half their property confiscated. Zubly appealed to the grand jury against this law, which he called an unconstitutional and tyrannical action by the new government. He refused to take an oath to the United States but was willing to take the required one to Georgia. This was of no avail, so he once more removed to South Carolina. He was included in the Georgia act of confiscation and banishment passed March 1, 1778, which confiscated all of his property. Zubly returned to British-held Savannah in the spring of 1781. He died there the following summer, still praying for king and country.

As set forth in his sermons and pamphlets, Zubly's ideas are a good example of American Whig thinking and constitutional argument prior to the Declaration of Independence. These ideas are in no sense weakened by the fact that Zubly refused to go along with independence. Zubly's personal tragedy in the Revolution well illustrates what happens to a person who is not willing to go all the way with revolutionary change and who lets public opinion get ahead of him. By insisting upon the same set of beliefs—rights of Englishmen within the empire—between 1765 and 1776 Zubly changed from a radical

Whig to a reactionary Tory, and from a leader in revolutionary thought to an opponent of revolt. Such is frequently the tragedy of loyalists in any revolution.

Kenneth Coleman
University of Georgia
January, 1972

The STAMP-ACT REPEALED;

A

SERMON,

Preached in the MEETING at SAVANNAH in GEORGIA, June 25th, 1766.

By J. J. ZUBLY, V. D. M.

Published at the Request and Expence of the Hearers.

Brethren, ye have been called unto liberty; only use not liberty as an occasion to the flesh.
But if ye bite and devour one another, take heed that ye be not consumed one of another. GALAT. v. 13, 15.

SAVANNAH: Printed by JAMES JOHNSTON.

M,DCC,LXVI.

To the
Rev: Mr Levi Hart

✦✦✦✦✦✦✦✦✦✦✦✦✦✦✦✦✦✦✦✦✦✦✦✦

Preston — Connecticut

Mr. *ZUBLY*'s

SERMON

ON THE

REPEAL

OF THE

STAMP-ACT.

✦✦✦✦✦✦✦✦✦✦✦✦✦✦✦✦✦✦✦✦✦✦✦✦

From your sincere Friend
and most obedient hum
Servant Thomas Bar

The STAMP-ACT REPEALED, *&c.*

TEXT. ZECHARIAH viii. 10, 11, 12.

*For before these days there was no hire for man, nor any
hire for beast; neither was there any peace to him that
went out, or came in, because of the affliction: for I set
all men every one against his neighbour. But now I will
not be unto the residue of this people as in the former
days, saith the* LORD *of hosts. For the seed shall be
prosperous: the vine shall give her fruit, and the
ground shall give her increase, and the heavens shall
give their dew: and I will cause the remnant of this
people to possess all these things.*

IT is remarkable that after *Israel* had conquered
all their enemies, and taken possession of the
land promised unto their fathers, they were very
near breaking out into a civil war among themselves, and no sooner were they freed of any appre-
hension from powerful and troublesome neighbours,
but the spirit of discord had well nigh succeeded in
transferring the seat of war into their own bowels.
We have an account of this important event in the
22d chapter of the Book of *Joshua*, and the sum of
it amounts to this: The tribes of *Reuben*, *Gad*, and
half the tribe of *Manasseh*, being settled on one, and
all the rest of the tribes on the other side of the
waters of *Jordan*, the former thought it necessary
to erect an altar on the borders of their frontier,

thereby

thereby to teftify that tho' *Jordan* was their boun-
dary, yet they were the fame people, united by the
fame ties, natural, religious & political, and that they
meant by this altar to inculcate and imprefs with
thefe fentiments the minds of their lateft pofterity.
The reft of the nation however took the alarm at
their proceedings, looked upon this as a ftep towards
independency, and feparation from the reft of their
brethren, and as they confidered the matter in this
view, it could not appear otherwife to them but exceeding alarming. Accordingly we are told, when
the children of *Ifrael* heard of it, the whole congregation gathered themfelves to go up to war againft
them; Jof. xxii. 12. their minds were thoroughly
enflamed, and every thing ready for blood and
flaughter. Among all this enraged multitude it feems
there were yet fome men of moderation, and their
lenient and healing counfels were the faving of the
people. Thefe tribes were but lately returned from
acting the part of faithful auxiliaries to their brethren; it was not at all probable that thofe meant to
feparate their interefts from that of the whole ftock,
who had given fuch fignal proofs of their attachment to the reft; before things are carried to the laft
extremity, a folemn meffage is fent to the fufpected
tribes, and when they came rightly to underftand
one another, the fidelity of the three diftinct tribes
fully appeared, and, inftead of looking upon them
as offenders, we are told their anfwer pleafed thofe
fent among them, *And* Phinehas *the fon of* Eleazar
the prieft faid unto the children of Reuben, *and to the*
children of Gad, *and to the children of* Manaffeh, *This*
day

day we perceive that the LORD *is among us, becaufe
ye have not committed this trefpafs againft the* LORD:
now ye have delivered the children of Ifrael *out of the
hand of the* LORD. *And* Phinehas *the fon of* Eleazar
*the prieft, and the princes, returned from the children
of* Reuben, *and from the children of* Gad, *out of the
land of* Gilead, *unto the land of* Canaan, *to the children of* Ifrael, *and brought them word again. And
the thing pleafed the children of* Ifrael; *and the children of* Ifrael *bleffed* GOD, *and did not intend to go up
againft them in battle, to deftroy the land wherein
the children of* Reuben *and* Gad *dwelt;* Jof. xxii.
31, 32, 33. The fpark which had like to kindle
fo great a fire was feafonably extinguifhed, a good
underftanding and mutual harmony reftored, every
man returned to his home and lived quietly under
his vine and fig-tree in the land which GOD had
fo lately givenunto them.

Methinks whoever perufes this account with attention may perceive fome paralell between the
cafe of *Ifrael* and what was lately our own. You
all know that for fome time paft the fituation between us and our brethren on the other fide of the
water has been exceeding alarming. Complaints
ran high, and it was even talked of that the ten
tribes intended to go to war againft their brethren,
and that notwithftanding during a very late war
thefe had given every poffible token of loyalty and
attachment. An unhappy ill-advifed act of the
Britifh legiflature laid the foundation of our griefs,
and it feemed as tho' the continuance of that act
and an univerfal alienation of minds muft go hand

in

in hand, the confequences of which might eafily be forefeen, they are not to be expreffed, becaufe they cannot be thought of without horror.

There were not wanting in *Britain*, nor yet in *America*, fome of the defcendants of the young counfellors of *Rehoboam* who would have convinced us of the juftice of that act by deadly arguments, and would not have been unwilling to fee *America* ruled with a rod of iron, but bleffed be GOD who defeated their counfels, who placed a king on the *Britifh* throne as tender of the liberty of the fubject as jealous of the glory of his own government; bleffed be GOD in whofe hands are the hearts of all men, that he inclined the *Britifh* parliament to hear the cries of the innocent, and, by a juft, noble, and generous repeal of that ill-concerted meafure, to diffipate our fears, remove our difficulties, reftore our confidence, to give us a pleafing opportunity to offer our publick thanks unto *Britain*'s GOD, and, like on the jubilee of old, to proclaim liberty throughout all the land to all the inhabitants thereof.

I do not know any event ever happened to *Britifh-America* more deferving of a publick day of thankfgiving throughout all that wide extended empire, and I would in the moft ferious manner call upon my congregation to offer thanks unto the Moft High, becaufe he has been favourable unto our land, and alfo to make a proper return to our moft gracious king, and the *Britifh* legiflature, for the removing of our fhoulders from the burden, and delivering our hands from the pots : *My heart*
is

is toward the governors of Ifrael *that offered them-*
felves willingly among the people. Bleſs ye the LORD.
They that were delivered from the noiſe of archers in the
places of drawing water; there ſhall they rehearſe the
righteous acts of the LORD, *even the righteous acts to-*
wards the inhabitants of his village in Iſrael: *then*
ſhall the people of the LORD *go down to the gates.*
Judges v. 9, 11.

The words which I have read unto you will af-
ford us ample matter for fuitable meditation on this
happy event; they are words of GOD himſelf, and
in their firſt intention are defigned to put *Ifrael* in
mind of the pleafing change of their publick affairs
from the time they had begun to lay the foundation
of the temple: Before that time we are told there
was no hire for man nor beaſt, no peace in all their
border, and the hand of GOD againſt them to vifit
them with fevere afflictions; and after that GOD
declares, that he will be no longer to them as in
days paſt, that now they may expect every kind of
bleffing, and that the remnant of the nation ſhould
henceforth poffefs and enjoy all thefe things.

As thefe words are expreffive of the gloomy ſtate
of the nation before that period, and the pleafing profpect now offered, they will want but
very little accommodation to our prefent purpofe.

My bufinefs therefore, under divine affiftance,
will be to

> Take fome notice of the day of *Jacob's* trouble,
> and the melancholy ſtate of the remnant of
> *Judah* while the hand of the LORD was a-
> gainſt them.

I

I would, in the next place, make a few remarks on the great and precious promifes
given unto the penitent remnant of the
Jewifh nation. And, laftly,

Endeavour to make fome improvement on the
whole fuitable to the defign of our prefent
meeting.

May I be enabled to fpeak on thefe things in a be-
coming manner, and may we not dare to put God
off with a little outward fhew, or the empty for-
mality of this meeting, but may we offer up foul
and body unto our fovereign benefactor and pre-
ferver; may this be the tribute of our gratitude and
our reafonable fervice!

Mercies received appear the greater when they
come after a long and painful want; the return of
the light is the more acceptable for the preceeding
darknefs; and fo God here puts them in mind of
the diftrefs under which they laboured till now,
that the promife of peace and plenty might be the
more welcome. If we confider the words in their
full extent they may lead us back to the ftate of
the nation at and during the invafion of the *Chaldeans*, and before *Judah* was carried into captivity;
then indeed there was no hire for man nor beaft,
no peace to him that came in nor went out: Befides the fcourge of war, *Judah* alfo fuffered by
drought and famine: Judah *mourneth, and the gates
thereof languifh: they are black unto the ground; becaufe the ground was chapt, for there was no rain in
the earth, the plowmen were afhamed, they covered
their heads.* Jer. xiv. 2, 4. All this calamity in-
creafed

creafed in proportion as the *Chaldeans* got the country in their poffeffion, and laid a clofe fiege to the
holy city and to their fanctuary. This mournful
defcription was more than once applicable to the
land of *Judah*, and it is mentioned as one of their
ufual afflictions when they departed from GOD;
In thofe times there was no peace to him that went out,
nor to him that came in, but great vexations were up-
on all the inhabitants of the countries, 2 Chron. xv. 5.
It is true indeed by this time the days of captivity
were accomplifhed, a number of them returned
to the land of their fathers, but even on their return their fituation was ftill deplorable, and their
difficulties exceeding great; *Jerufalem* was a heap
of ftones, and all the country around a mere defo-
lation; they met with oppofition from the *Sama-*
ritans, and all their afflictions had not yet made
them wife enough to agree among themfelves; their
neglect alfo in building the houfe of GOD had
brought on them very fevere judgments; they looked for much and it came to little, and when they
brought even that little home GOD did blow upon
it; when a man came to an heap of twenty meafures there were but ten, and when one came to
the wine prefs to draw out fifty veffels there were
but twenty, and all this becaufe the houfe of the
LORD lay wafte, and every man ran to his own
houfe; *Haggai i. 9. ii. 16.* Such was their wretched ftate at the time of this prophecy, and how
wretched muft a people be where there is no hire
for man nor beaft, no peace in coming in and going
out, and where the judgments of GOD fet every

B   man

man againſt his neighbour in the greatneſs of the affliction.

When there is no hire for man or beaſt, it is a plain ſign that buſineſs is at a ſtand, and every ſtagnation of this kind threatens the very vitals of a country. This calamity falls heavieſt upon the lower and middling claſs of people, who make up the body and the moſt uſeful part of every nation. When the fields lie waſte, the huſbandman mourneth, the neceſſaries of life are with difficulty procured by the rich, and hunger and want ſeem unavoidable to the poor; ſometimes when the multitude of inhabitants is greater than the land can bear, even the induſtrious cannot long find employ, and for want of that are reduced to diſtreſs; ſometimes when by war and other devaſtations countries are ſo drained that labourers are not to be had, a man is more precious than fine gold, yea than the golden wedge of ophir; *Iſaiah xiii.* 12. Though theſe caſes be oppoſite yet the effect is the ſame; neither does it affect thoſe only who are more immediate ſufferers; the rich cannot live without the poor, and he that hires cannot do without ſome one to hire. Trade may indeed ſupply the wants of a nation, but trade is only an artificial ſupply; a country that has room for the ſpreading of its inhabitants, and has ground for tillage proportionable to their increaſe, muſt have greatly the advantage over a mere trading nation; the former can find thoſe reſources within itſelf for which the latter muſt be indebted to trade with its colonies and other nations. The gains of trade
may

may possibly be larger than those by cultivation, but a country well cultivated will always nourish and maintain its inhabitants, a country blessed with natural advantages will easily procure the conveniencies and even superfluities of life, either within itself, or at least by the exports of its natural produce; *The profit of the earth is for all, even the king himself is served by the field;* Ecclef. v. 9. but when there is no hire neither for man nor beast, it is a sure sign that cultivation and trade is languishing, and it is with bodies politick as it is with the natural body when once they begin to languish, if a remedy is not speedily found out and adhibited, it must affect every part of the whole, and the whole gradually fall into decay and consumption.

This was the case of the small remnant left in *Canaan*; they were only some of the meanest of the people, husbandmen and dressers of vineyards, and it seems probable that even these were rather slaves than subjects to the king of *Babylon*; hence they complain that they are servants in their own land, *Neb.* ix. 36. *Our inheritance is turned to strangers, our houses to aliens. Our necks are under persecution: we labour, and have no rest;* Lam. v. 2, 5.

During all these disasters, it was doubtless an additional and severe affliction, *that there was no peace to him that came in nor went out;* those that were already captives in *Babylon* could not with any safety return into their own land, and they that were left in it, and fain wanted to retire into *Egypt*, or any other place of security, could not go out; and even among themselves there was no

B 2   peace,

peace, no unanimity, but continual jarrings and dif-
cords. Some very remarkable inftances of the kind
are mentioned in the forty-firft chapter of *Jeremi-
ah*; even after their return all things were fo unfet-
tled, that, notwithftanding the hopeful appearance
of their being once more reftored to their own land,
there was no peace to him that came in nor to him
that went out; this was little better than war, and

War in its beft light is a deftruction of the human fpecies, but war among brethren, inteftine
feuds and civil wars as they are called, of the worft
evil are the worft fpecies; when the right hand is
lifted up againft the left, when the members of the
fame body feek each other's deftruction, the whole
body muft needs feel, and if they continue, be deftroyed by it. And here I cannot but remember the
addrefs made by fome general to an *Abyffinian* monarch, who could imagine it worth his while to go
to war with his own fubjects, in order to make
them fubmit to fome religious rites and ceremonies,
which he thought himfelf in confcience bound to
impofe upon them, and which they thought themfelves in confcience bound to fuffer any hardfhip
rather than fubmit unto; a battle was fought, the
prince was victorious, the field covered with the
flain, when the general thus addreffed the conquer-
ing monarch, pointing at the heaps of the flaugh-
tered; " Thefe were your own fubjects, and in e-
" very other caufe willing to fhed their blood and
" lay down their lives for you---they were our bre-
" thren, our own flefh and blood, and every vic-
" tory of the kind you gain over them is a ftep
" to-

" towards the entire ruin of your own nation."
Methinks the warrior that fpoke fo, fpoke like a
fenfible man and good patriot. The king gained
the battle and gave up the point, wifely confider-
ing, that the gaining the affection of loyal fubjects
would be a greater fecurity to his reign and kingdom than any fubmiffion he could force them unto
by any act of mere power.

Union of minds and interefts is the real ftrength
of any nation, a kingdom divided againft itfelf cannot ftand; *Ifrael* fell indeed by the fword of the
Chaldeans, but their own internal divifions gave the
finithing ftroke; the diftrefs which they had
brought upon themfelves was great exceedingly,
the hand of the LORD was ftretched out againft
them, and the people returned not to him who did
fmite them; their affliction, inftead of humbling
them before GOD, only ferved to heighten their
animofities againft one another; their affliction is
exprefsly mentioned as the caufe of their difturban-
ces, they hated, miftrufted, fupplanted one another, and therefore there was no peace to him that
came in, nor yet to him that went out.

There was no peace to him that came in, nor to
him that went out, *becaufe of the affliction.* When
people think they have nothing more to hope they
are apt to conclude they have alfo nothing to fear.
When tyranny and oppreffion once arrive at a certain height, they become intolerable even to loyalty, and muft recoil upon their authors. It is
dangerous for fovereigns to make the experiment,
how much their fubjects may be able and willing

to bear. Oppreffion makes even a wife man mad, and when any kingdom is all in confufion within itfelf, when violence beareth rule, and the good of the community ceafes to be the fupreme law, when unreafonable burdens are laid upon fome to procure eafe unto others, when jarring interefts and different factions divide the ftate and impofe upon the fovereign, fuch a nation not only ceafes to be formidable to its neighbours and enemies, but it is alfo in very great danger of falling into the condition within itfelf which is here defcribed, no peace to him that goes out nor to him that comes in.

Neither do all thefe things fpring up out of the duft, or come upon a people by chance, or in the common courfe of things: *Shall there be evil in the city, and the* LORD *hath not done it?* Amos iii. 6. GOD indeed *is not the author of confufion but of peace*, 1 Cor. xiv. 33. he does not love iniquity but he alfo hateth oppreffion. Sometimes the fins of the fubject are punifhed by arbitrary fovereigns, and oppreffion and arbitrary power are fometimes vifited (and overfet too) by the violence of unruly fubjects.

There is a very remarkable inftance of this in the reign of the fon of *Salomon*. He came to the throne by hereditary right, unhappily for him he and his council probably thought that right indefeafible, his father had made his yoke heavy upon the land, at his acceffion to the throne, the fubjects modeftly reprefent their grievance, the fons of violence reject the moderate requeft of the fons of juft and decent freedom, a tax, till then unheard of it would feem, is impofed, an
officer

officer is fent to gather the odious tribute, but the
officer, by the verdict of all *Ifrael*, is ftoned with
ftones, the king himfelf retires with precipitation,
a war is refolved on, one hundred fourfcore thoufand men take up arms againft *Ifrael*, and appear
ready to fall on; but the word of GOD came unto
Shemaiah, the man of GOD, faying, Speak unto
Rehoboam, the fon of *Salomon* king of *Judah*, and
unto all the houfe of *Judah* and *Benjamin*, and to
the remnant of the people, faying, Thus faith the
LORD, ye fhall not go up, nor fight againft your
brethren the children of *Ifrael*; return every man to
his houfe, for this thing is of me, faith the LORD.
And we are further told, they hearkened therefore
to the word of the LORD, and returned to depart according to the word of the LORD ; thus the fhed-
ding of blood was at that time prevented, and a ftop
put to a cruel and inteftine war by an immediate
interpofition of divine providence, and that at the
expence of *Rehoboam*, who was never able to bring
back the ten tribes, but they continued a feparate
kingdom till they fell into the hands of their common enemy.

I do not mention all this to juftify or approve in
every refpect the conduct of the ten tribes, but to
obferve that if *Rehoboam* had taken the falutary advice
of his old prudent counfellors, the defection and en-
fuing divifion would not have happened. [1 *Kings*
xii. throughout.]

GOD cannot delight in, blefs, or approve any
thing that is wicked: *Though hand join in hand, the*
wicked fhall not be unpunifhed, Prov. xi. 21. Oppreffion

preſſion and rebellion are both wicked, and may
become by a righteous judgment of God a ſcourge
to one another. God abhors ſin and evil, but even
ſin and evil is not committed without his knowledge and ſufferance; he forms the light and creates darkneſs, he makes peace and creates evil, he
the Lord does all theſe things; *Iſaiah xlv. 7.* His
wiſdom and juſtice in ſome caſes may permit the
peace and tranquility of a ſinful nation to be inter-
rupted or taken away, by ſuffering the rulers to be
intoxicated with too high notions of power, or by
ſuffering the ſubjects to go beyond the juſt bounds,
in aſſerting and maintaining their juſt rights, and
confuſion and diſorders are the natural effects of all
this, and it is as natural a conſequence that in thoſe
days there is no hire for man nor beaſt, no peace to
him that goes out nor comes in, and that every
man is againſt his neighbour on account of the affliction.

Thus far the gloomy part; let us next take notice
of the pleaſing proſpect that opens by the change of
the ſcene and the divine promiſe.

What God himſelf marks out as a very ſignal divine bleſſing, men certainly ſhould receive as a precious mark of his favour. To remove ſo great an
affliction, and to change their mournful condition
into peace, plenty, and liberty, muſt be unto them
an irreſiſtible proof that God was again returned
unto them in mercy; and this indeed he aſſures
them of in expreſs words: *I will not be unto the re-
ſidue of my people as in former days, ſaith the Lord
of hoſts; for the ſeed ſhall be proſperous, the vine ſhall
give*

*give her fruit, and the ground shall give her increase,
and the heavens shall give their dew, and I will make
the remnant of my people to possess all these things.*

Here is a general promise that God would not
deal with them as he had of late. God changeth
not neither in his nature or purposes; there is no
shadow with him of variableness or turning; but
there is a connection between man's carriage towards God and the way of God towards man:
*The Lord is with you, if ye be with him; and if ye
seek him, he will be found of you; but if ye forsake
him, he will forsake you;* 2 Chron. xv. 2. With
the pure he shews himself pure; and in this sense
it is said, that with the froward he will shew himself froward; *Psalm xviii.* 26. National sins bring
on national calamities, and national reformation a
national blessing; the same God that threatens to
pluck up, pull down, and destroy a rebellious
kingdom, will also turn from the evil he has threatened when they return from the evil which they
have committed; and that this was the case at this
time in *Israel* appears plain from the prayers of
Daniel, Ezra, Nehemiah, and many others; while
they continued rebellious, the hand of the Lord
should continue to be heavy upon them, but now
they returned unto God, he would return unto
them in mercy.

The labourer and husbandman should now be
employed, the fields should be cultivated, and in
the land that lay desolate, and almost uninhabited,
in the land that was without man or beast, fields
should be bought again for money, and there

C   should

should be hire for man and beast; *Jerusalem* should *be inhabited as towns without walls, for the multitude of men and cattle therein*, Zech. ii. 4.

Their coming in and their going out should be in peace, he should strengthen the bars of their gates, and give peace unto their borders.

They should no longer be a disunited nation, but unite like the heart of one man; *I will* (saith GOD) *give them one heart and one way, that they may fear me for ever, for the good of them and of their children after them*, Jer. xxxii. 39.

Neither does GOD only promise a removal of those evils under which in former days they groaned, but there is life also in his favour; GOD in his very nature is kind unto all, and his tender mercies are over all the works of his hands. Nothing but mercy would always attend man, had not man turned away from the love of his maker. Sin only makes a separation between us and our GOD, and when the cause of his displeasure is removed, the streams of his kindness follow their natural course, and flow down upon man. The order and œconomy of the whole creation speaks aloud the kind designs of GOD to man; fury is not in him; punishing is his strange and the doing kindness is his natural work: Accordingly on their being turned unto him, and he unto them, he promises them the very reverse of the evils under which they had hitherto laboured; plenty instead of famine, the dew of heaven and rain in due season instead of drought, and every kind of temporal prosperity and abundance in the land to which they were now

restored;

reſtored; the heavens ſhould not be of braſs, nor
the earth of iron; God would no longer forbid the
clouds to rain upon them, but he would hear the
heavens, and they ſhould hear the earth, and the
earth ſhould hear corn, wine, and oil, and theſe
ſhould hear *Jezreel, Hoſea ii.* 21, 22. Neither
ſhould theſe bleſſings be only tranſitory but dur-
able, the days of their mourning ſhould be at an
end, and the remnant of the nation now returned
unto the Lord and to his ſanctuary ſnould rejoice
in the poſſeſſion of all theſe bleſſings; they ſhould
no longer hang up their harps by the willows, but
again ſing the ſongs of *Sion* in their own land, and
give thanks unto the Lord, who had brought them
again from the heathen, and turned their captivity
like the ſtreams in the ſouth: *O* Lord, *I will praiſe
thee; though thou waſt angry with me, thine anger is
turned away, and thou comfortedſt me. Cry out and
ſhout, thou inhabitant of* Zion; *for great is the holy
one of* Iſrael *in the midſt of thee;* Iſaiah xii. 1, 6.

And this naturally leads me, which was the laſt
thing propoſed, to endeavour an improvement of
what has been ſaid ſuitable to the deſign of our
preſent meeting.

Some among us poſſibly may be ready to aſk,
what meaneth this ſervice, it is neither *Sabbath*
nor new moon. To them I would anſwer: We
are met to-day to offer our thanks unto the great
ruler of all things, that he has averted from us a
very great evil, which in part indeed was come
upon us already, and which, conſidered as a puniſh-
ment of our ſins, we but too juſtly deſerve.

C 2   We

We are met to offer thanks unto GOD, that our invaluable privileges are preferved, that our land is not become a land of flaves, nor our fields a fcene of blood. We are met to give thanks unto GOD, that our gloomy apprehenfions are removed, that the *Britifh* parliament has feen the juftice of our complaints, that our fuperiors, by this act of juftice and moderation, have fhewn themfelves fuperior to themfelves. We rejoice that affection and confidence is reftored between us and our mother country. We are met to give thanks unto the Moft High, that, by the repeal of this act, there is hire again for man and beaft, that our ports are open, our trade unmolefted, that we may go to and fro in fafety, that men are no more fet every man againft his neighbour, that *Manaffeh* is not againft *Ephraim*, nor *Ephraim* againft *Manaffeh*; and we are alfo met to pray, that our pofterity may enjoy all thefe things, that mercy and truth may be the bleffing of our days, and of our whole nation, and that our civil and religious liberties may be preferved inviolable till time fhall be no more.

I fuppofe there are few or none hearing me that think we have not now any particular caufe to be thankful; if any fhould think fo, I fhould defpair of convincing them that we really have; it is generally obferved, that we beft know to value our mercies from the want of them, but I fincerely wifh there may never be any conviction of this kind in all the *Britifh* dominions.

Come then, my friends, let us make mention of the mercies of the LORD according to all his goodnefs,

nefs, and according to the multitude of his loving-kindneffes which he has fhewn unto the *Britifh* nation. Your own minds will too eafily fuggeft unto you what muft have been our cafe if this unhappy act had not been repealed; and fhould not our gratitude bear fome proportion to the greatnefs of our efcape? Should we not thankfully review every circumftance that brought about this pleafing event, and offer our humble and fincere thanks to the kind providence of God, that gave fuccefs to the noble and unwearied endeavours of our friends for that purpofe? I think the almoft unanimous, fteady, and prudent union of the *Americans*, does honour to their prefent generation, and as it was very providential, and to many I fuppofe very unexpected, fo I look upon it as a real matter of gratitude. I would not be underftood to vindicate every thing that a confufed multitude or a few individuals may have done in a time of publick confufion, but the manly, nervous, and conftitutional reprefentations made by the reprefentatives of the people, may be looked upon as one of the means which providence has made ufe of to fet the juftice of the *American* complaints in its true light, and to excite us able and worthy friends to ftand up as noble champions for our caufe. Had a whole people, who looked upon themfelves as oppreffed and dealt with contrary to their natural privileges, been difregarded, there is no faying what might have been the confequence; and the confequence muft have been felt on each fide of the water; we muft fink or fwim together. That all our fears

have

have fubfided, that all this jealoufy has been removed, in the dark night which feemed to hang
over our heads is turned into the light of a hopeful
morning, furely calls for our loudeft and fincereft
thankfgiving : Offer therefore unto GOD thanks,
give unto the LORD glory and ftrength, let thofe
that cried unto the LORD in trouble, and he faved
them out of their diftreffes, give thanks unto his
name. *He brought them out of darknefs, and the fhadow of death, and brake their bands in funder. Oh,
that men would praife the* LORD *for his goodnefs, and
for his wonderful works to the children of men!* Pfalm
cvii. 14, 15.

And, in the next place, let our thanks be given
to our great and good King, the friend of mankind, and the father of his people. He glories to
reign in the hearts of his fubjeds; and no king can
have a better title to the hearts of thofe over whom
he rules. If it is *a pleafure to him* to repeal an ad
that gives pain unto his fubjeds, may all his fervants copy after him, and ad worthy of the principles of fo great a king, and fo good a mafter;
and may every poffible demonftration of loyalty and
affedion be ever paid him by all, but efpecially by
his *American* fubjeds. The *Americans,* who, I
believe I may juftly fay to a man, have been
friends to the fucceffion in his illuftrious houfe, if
poffible, muft now fhew a ftill greater degree of
attachment in return for this royal condefcenfion
and favour.

  Blefs, O GOD, the king; long let the crown
flourifh on his head. Give him the defires
of

of his foul; may he ever be a king after thine own heart; give him wife counfellors and faithful fubjects; let his reign be long, peaceable, and glorious; may the wicked never ftand before his throne, and fo his throne be ever eftablifhed in righteoufnefs; and may our pofterity in fome diftant generation pay him the mournful tear, when he is taken up into a kingdom that cannot be fhaken.

Let me further befeech you, my hearers, to remember the rock from which you were hewn; by defcent or incorporation we are now all *Britons*; let *Britain*'s interefts be ever dear to us all. Pray for the profperity of the nation, for in her profperity you fhall profper. We have feen our mothercountry act the part of a tender parent; let us never fail to act the part of truly dutiful children. May *Britons* have a love for one another which many waters cannot quench. May eaftern and weftern *Britons* ever be more firmly united than *Jofeph* and *Ephraim*, which were made like one ftick in the hands of the prophet. If GOD abhors him who foweth difcord among brethren, let us abhor them who would do any thing that might tend towards a feparation of interefts or an alienation of affections. Let *Britain* and *Britifh America* ever be like one heart and one foul; he that would divide them, *anathema fit*, let him be held accurfed by both.

It is a remark of the wifeft king, *Evil men underftand not judgment, but they that fear the* LORD *under-*

understand [take notice of, observe, and improve] *all things,* Prov. xxviii. 5. Let us remember then, and let our posterity know it, that if a prudent, proper remonstrance had not been made and received, the year 1765 must have been the fatal year from which the loss of *American* liberty must have been dated. Let us also remember, that the year following was remarkable for the repeal of an act that gave so universal uneasiness, and had like to be so destructive to *Britain* on each side of the great waters. *

If we record these remarkable interesting events, it may not be improper to subjoin: Fear GOD, honour the king, stand fast in your liberty, and be not entangled with the yoke of bondage.

Let us forgive our enemies and honour our friends, the more so because some of them (which is a pleasing honourable circumstance) have at all times signally distinguished themselves in the cause of liberty, and deserved greatly of the *British* nation. Let every injury received be written in sand, and all kindness be preserved in marble, and every friend of liberty and his country be held in everlasting remembrance.

The design of the repeal was to remove inconveniencies and consequences detrimental to the
British

The Stamp-Act was to have taken place Nov. 1, 1765, and it took place in all provinces *conquered* from the French and Spaniards in the last war, also in most of the islands, the military government of Nova Scotia; and in Georgia stamps were   for shipping only. The said act was repealed in the house of commons by a majority of 108, and a majority of 34 in the house of Lords; and the repealing act received the royal assent March 18, 1766.

British kingdoms; let us then do nothing which might continue thofe inconveniencies which that wife and falutary act means to prevent.

Efpecially let us never give any handle to any to call in queftion our loyalty to the king, and our fincere and firm atta.. ment to our mother-country; let us ever be zealous for its profperity, and promote it to the utmoft of ov power; let each one of us fay upon this occafion: *Pray for the peace of* Britain ; *they fhall profper that love thee. Peace be within thy walls, and profperity within thy palaces. For my brethren and companions fakes I will now fay, Peace* unto *thee. Becaufe of the houfe of the* LORD *our* GOD *I will feek thy good*; Pfalm cxxii. 6, 7, 8, 9. Let us pay a chearful obedience to the laws of the realm, and on all occafions approve ourfelves worthy fubjects of the beft of kings. Let us always return a filial refpect to the indulgence and tendernefs of an affectionate parent. Let us convince even thofe who have taken upon them to vilify and mifreprefent the *Americans* how greatly they have been miftaken, and how very unjuft have been their inflammatory reflections. Let the mean tools of faction be put to fhame, (if they are capable of that) by a conduct the very reverfe of that which they would have laid to our charge. Let us by well-doing put to filence the ignorance or malice of foolifh or wicked men. Let every diftinction of names and parties, every national prejudice, be buried in everlafting oblivion. Let the good man whoever he be be the object of univerfal love and efteem, and the bad man the only object of aver-

fion

sion and abhorrence. Let there be no other emulation but who shall best promote the good of the whole. Render to every one his due, tribute to whom tribute, custom to whom custom, fear to whom fear, honour to whom honour. *Submit yourselves to every ordinance of man for the* LORD's *sake, whether it be to the king as supreme; Or unto governors, as unto them that are sent by him for the punishment of evil-doers, and for the praise of them that do well: As free, and not using your liberty for a cloke of maliciousness, but as the servants of* GOD; 1 Peter ii. 13, 14, 16. There is a very essential difference between liberty and licentiousness, and it is highly criminal under pretence of the one to indulge the other. If any excess of this kind has been committed, may it be sincerely repented of and carefully avoided for the future, *so speak and so act as they that shall be judged by the law of liberty*, James ii. 13.

ABOVE ALL, let us ever remember, that *righteousness exalteth a nation, but sin is a reproach to any people*, Prov. xiv. 34. Our temporal happiness cannot be more surely promoted, nor our civil and religious liberties be better secured, than by a life suitable to the dignity of our christian profession. Christianity is a benevolent institution, that bears a friendly aspect to civil government, and does not in the least diminish the natural or civil rights of the subject. It teaches superiors to rule in the fear of GOD, and to look upon their subjects as their fellow creatures and brethren, whose happiness to promote is the very design of their office; it engages subjects to obey for the LORD's sake, not only

to

to the gentle but also to the froward. We cannot
be good christians unless we are also good subjects
and good members of the community; let every one
then depart from iniquity that is named after *Christ.*
By promoting our eternal we also shall secure our
temporal welfare; nothing that has a tendency to
make us unhappy hereafter can have any tendency
to make us happy here. If ever (which GOD forbid) we should be cursed with a tyrannical oppressive government, our sins must be the cause of it.
O! let us not sin away our mercies, neither let us
sin any more left something worse befal us. We
can never be said to be free while we are the
servants of sin, neither can any bondage equal that
of being led captive by *Satan* according to his will;
and yet this is the case of every graceless sinner,
While they promise them *liberty, they themselves are
the servants of corruption: for of whom a man is overcome, of the same is he brought into bondage,* 2 Peter
ii. 19. How insignificant will our struggle for liberty appear, while we deliberately give up ourselves to be slaves unto lust; if we abhor bondage,
O! let us at least take care that our bondage may
not be eternal; chains of eternal darkness are the
portion of every impenitent sinner; and *Know ye
not that to whom ye yield yourselves to obey, his servants
ye are to whom ye obey, whether of sin unto death, or
of obedience unto righteousness?* Rom. vi. 16. When
will the poor captive begin to feel his fetters and
groan for liberty? Where the spirit of the LORD is
there is liberty, and where the spirit of the world
and sin reigns there is slavery and bondage. Every

de-

deliberate fin helps to rivet the chain, and the longer vicious habits are indulged the more difficult it
is to fhake off their dominion. Man was made free,
but he alfo was made good; the finner has loft his
original goodnefs, and liberty departed from him,
when he hearkened to the voice of the tempter; one
cannot be recovered without the other; if we will
be truly free we muft become truly good; we muft
be renewed in the fpirit of our mind, and be created after GOD in righteoufnefs and true holinefs,
Eph. iv. 24. This, my hearers, is the true idea of
liberty, to be freed from every hurtful conftraint,
and to be able to do all that tends to make us truly
happy, or elfe to be free indeed is neither more nor
lefs than to be heartily engaged for him whofe fervice is perfect freedom.

O! my hearers, with what pleafure did we lately
receive the news which makes the fubject of our
thankfgiving to-day, how did joy fparkle in every
countenance, how warmly did we fhake hands and
congratulate one another upon the occafion; we
feemed like people that had been apprehenfive of
being fhipwrecked and happily made a harbour;
we feemed almoft like animals in the air pump to
whom breath and life is reftored by the return of
that element; never before have I feen any news
received with equal and fo univerfal fatisfaction;
and all that was right; there were reafons more
than fufficient for great fear, and when they fubfided it was meet they fhould be fucceeded by joy
as great: But with what woeful coldnefs and indifference have too many carried themfelves towards
the

the beſt news that was ever ſent from heaven upon earth; how little have we been affected with the glad tidings of great joy, that unto us is a ſaviour born. *Jeſus Chriſt* himſelf came to preach deliverance to the captives, to ſet at liberty them that were bruiſed, to preach the acceptable year of the Lord; he was in bonds that he might break our chains, he laid down his life as a ranſom for thoſe that were in bondage of *Satan* and ſin, he died that we might eternally live. Our king is alſo our ſaviour, his ſubjects are the purchaſe of his blood, and he invites ſtrangers to come and kiſs his ſceptre, with no other view but that he may have the pleaſure of making them eternally happy. Behold how much has he loved us, and how ſhall we now eſcape if we neglect his great ſalvation? How ungrateful are we to him, and how unjuſt to ourſelves, if we chuſe to continue in that ſlavery which he has been at ſuch amazing pains to redeem us from.

Come then, my friends, let us embrace this opportunity and become his real ſubjects; let us chearfully forſake the ſervice of vanity and ſin, and unreſervedly give ourſelves up to the Lord that bought us. How happy would it be, if from this pleaſing event we might alſo date our ſincere and hearty endeavours at leaſt, to become his freemen, that, being delivered from the fear of our enemies, we might ſerve him *in holineſs and righteouſneſs all the days of our life*, Luke i. 75. then, and not till then, ſhall we be a people really free and truly happy; then will the ſon make us free, and we ſhall
be

be free indeed; then fhall we have a moft indifputable right to the glorious liberty of the fons of GOD.

When fhall the kingdom of *Chrift* extend over all the earth, and homage be paid him by thofe who fit now in darknefs and in the fhadow of death? When fhall his gentle reign be the blifs of every nation, ignorance, flavery, and fuperftition, be altogether banifhed from the earth, and the bleffings of peace, liberty, and the gofpel, be fcattered over the whole wide creation?

For thefe things, my brethren, let us pray, thy kingdom come, and feeing we look for a kingdom that cannot be fhaken, let us by faith and holinefs be daily preparing for the fame; there the wicked ceafe from troubling and the weary are at reft.

Now to the King invifible, immortal, and eternal, to him who is able to keep us, and to prefent us before GOD with exceeding great joy, to the only wife GOD our faviour, be glory and majefty, dominion and power, both now and ever. AMEN.

Savannah
in
Georgia

July 23 1766

A N

HUMBLE ENQUIRY

I N T O

The NATURE of the DEPENDENCY of the
AMERICAN COLONIES upon the PAR-
LIAMENT of *GREAT-BRITAIN*,

A N D

The RIGHT of PARLIAMENT to lay TAXES
on the said COLONIES.

By a FREEHOLDER of *SOUTH-CAROLINA.*

A House divided against itself cannot stand.

When people heard ship money demanded *as a right*, and found it by sworn judges of the law adjudged so, upon such grounds and reasons as every stander-by was able to swear was not law, and so had lost the pleasure and delight of being kind and dutiful to the King, and, instead of GIVING, were required to PAY, and by a logick that left no man any thing that he might call his own, they no more looked upon it as the case of one man, but the case of the kingdom, nor as an imposition laid upon them by the King, but by the judges, which they thought themselves bound in publick justice not to submit to. It was an observation long ago of *Thucydides*, "That men are much more passionate for injustice " than for violence, because (saith he) the one proceeding as from an equal seems " rapine, when the other proceeding from a stranger is but the effect of necessity." —When they saw reason of state urged as elements of law, judges as sharp-sighted as secretaries of state, judgment of law grounded upon matter of fact of which there was neither, enquiry nor proof, and no reason given for the payment but what included all the estates of the standers by, they had no reason to hope that doctrine, or the promoters of it, would be contained within any bounds; and it is no wonder that they who had so little reason to be pleased with their own condition were no less solicitous for, or apprehensive of the inconveniences that might attend any alteration.—*History of the long Rebellion, Vol. 1. p. 70, 71.*

PRINTED in the YEAR M,DCC,LXIX.

[Price Twelve Shillings and Sixpence.]

AN HUMBLE ENQUIRY, &c.

THOUGH few or none claim infallibility in exprefs terms, yet it is very difficult ever to perfuade fome men they are miftaken. We generally have fo good an opinion of our own underftanding, that infenfibly we take it for granted thofe that do not think as we do muft needs be in the wrong. When difputes are once heightened by perfonal prejudice, or the bitternefs of party, it becomes fo much the more difficult to the difputants themfelves to fee their miftakes, and even to byftanders the truth appears wrapped up in a cloud, and through the fog and duft of argument becomes almoft imperceptible.

Thefe remarks I believe will particularly hold good in the fubject now in agitation between *Great-Britain* and her colonies, a fubject however of too ferious a nature to be given up to prejudice, or to be decided by the rage of party. Every argument *pro* or *con* deferves to be moft carefully weighed, and he that fets the whole in the cleareft light does the publick no inconfiderable fervice, and that whether it be by pointing out the juftice of the *American* claims to *Great-Britain*, or fetting fuch conftitutional arguments before the *Americans* as muft either leave obftinacy inexcufable, or will difpofe loyal and reafonable men to a chearful acquiefcence.

The argument on which the *Americans* feem to lay the greateft ftrefs is, they fay that it is a principle of the *Britifh* conftitution, that no *Englifhman* ought to be taxed but by his own confent, given either by himfelf or his reprefentative. I find it admitted by fuch as difapprove the *American* claims, that no man is bound by any law to which he hath not given his confent either in perfon or by a reprefentative. Perhaps thefe two propofitions are not perfectly equivalent; however it feems clear, that he that holds that no man is bound BY ANY LAW to which he hath not perfonally or by a reprefentative confented, muft alfo admit, that no man is bound by any law that lays a tax on him without his confent given by himfelf or reprefentative. What is true of ALL laws in general muft alfo hold true of EVERY law in particular. If no law can operate upon any man that hath not in the above manner given his affent to

A   it, it, certainly no fuch law can be binding upon whole communities, or any confiderable part of the whole nation. In the fpirit of the above principle, it feems effential to law, that it be affented to by fuch on whom it is afterwards to operate. To fuppofe, therefore, that a law is binding upon fuch as have not given their affent, is to fuppofe (I argue upon that principle) a law may be valid and binding at the fame time it is confeffedly deftitute of the very effential point to make it fo; and if the affent of thofe that are to be governed by the law is not neceffary or effential to the making of it, then reprefentation is a mere fuperfluous thing, no better than an extrefcence in the legiflative power, which therefore at any convenient time may be lopped off at pleafure, and without the leaft danger to the conftitution; the governed then have no part in the legiflation at all, the will of thofe in power, whoever they be, is the fupreme and fole law, and what hath been above afferted to be a conftitutional principle feems to me to fall to the ground without remedy to all intents and purpofes.

Suppofing, on the other hand, that principle, as is afferted to be conftitutional, then to me, as is further afferted, it feems to be of the very nature of it, that it be general and hold in all cafes. This it does not only clearly imply, but alfo fully and ftrongly exprefs; but yet if fo, it would alfo feem that no man, or no people, in no cafe, or by no power whatever, can be bound to pay a tax to which they have not confented either perfonally or by their reprefentatives. Every conftitutional principle muft be general and hold in all cafes, and I may add in all places too, for it is ufually faid that the liberties of an *Englifhman* follow him to the end of the world, much more then muft they follow him over all the *Britifh* dominions; this is fo true, that by an exprefs law, the children of *Britifh* parents, though born in a foreign dominion, are juft as much entitled to all *Britifh* liberties as thofe who have been born within the realm.

An inference may poffibly hence be drawn, that if fo, the *Britifh* colonies are fubject to none of the acts of the *Britifh* Parliament, (*fcil.* becaufe they never affented to them neither in perfon nor by reprefentative) and therefore muft be confidered as independent of the legal or parliamentary power of *Great-Britain.* I confefs I fhould be forry to fee *America* independent of *Great-Britain*, and if any of the arguments the *Americans* make ufe of imply an independency on the mother ftate, I fhould fhrewdly fufpect there muft be fome fallacy couched under an otherwife fpecious appearance. The fum and ftrength of this inference I conceive lies thus: The *Britifh* legiflature muft be the fupreme power in all the *Britifh* dominions, and if fo, all the *Britifh* dominions ought to pay obedience in all cafes to all the laws in which they are mentioned that may be enacted

acted by the *British* Parliament, and to refuse obedience in any such
case is to declare themselves an independent people.

I freely own I have not heard any thing stronger said in favour
of taxation by the *British* Parliament, and I think this argument is
highly deserving the most serious confideration. Every good man
would wish to hear the voice of di passionate reason before he forms
his judgment in any debate. Vulgar prejudices may sway vulgar
minds but a wise man is neither carried away by the torrent of
power, nor the blaft of popularity. I would endeavour therefore
to confider this argument with all the candour and impartiality I
am capable of; I would do it with a mind open to conviction, and
with steadiness fufficient to follow truth wherever she may lead me.

To have a clear view how far this argument may affect the prefent queftion between *Great-Britain* and her colonies, it will be necessary carefully to ftate the relation which they bear to one another; without this we shall never have a precife and determinate
idea of the matter. The argument I think is made up of two pro-
positions, *viz.*

The Parliament of *Great-Britain* is the supreme legiflature in all
the *British* empire.

All the *British* dominions therefore ought to pay obedience thereto in all cafes and to all the laws in which they are mentioned,
and to refufe obedience to any fuch is to declare themfelves an
independent people.

Before I proceed to take a diftinct view of each of thefe propofitions, I repeat, that they are faid to be built upon a conftitutional
principle, and that this principle muft be general and hold in all
cafes; this muft undoubtedly be admitted, for what enters into
the very effence of the conftitution muft doubtlefs operate as far as
the conftitution itfelf. Let us now proceed to confider every part
of thefe two propofitions diftinctly, and this muft infallibly lead us
to form a found judgment of the whole.

The kingdom of GREAT BRITAIN confifts of two parts, north and
fouth, or *England* and *Scotland*, united fince 1707 into one kingdom,
under the name of *Great-Britain*. This union hath not been fo full
and abfolute, as to put both kingdoms in all refpects upon a perfect
equality; but tho' the legiflature is the fame, yet the laws and the
adminiftration of juftice are not the fame in every inftance. The
fame legiflature making laws that affect only the one or the other
of thefe kingdoms, and even laws made to be binding upon both,
do not affect both alike, of which the difference in raifing the fupplies by land tax is a very full and ftriking proof, this could not be
the cafe if the union between the two kingdoms was fo entire and
abfolute, as for inftance between *England* and the principality of
Wales.

The BRITISH EMPIRE is a more extenfive word, and should not
be

be confounded with the kingdom of *Great-Britain*; it confifts of *England, Scotland, Ireland,* the Iflands of *Man, Jerfey, Guernfey, Gibraltar,* and *Minorca, &c.* in the *Mediterranean* ; *Senegal, &c.* in *Africa*; *Bombay, &c.* in the *Eaft-Indies*; and the Iflands and Colonies in *North-America, &c.* As *England,* ftrictly fo called, is at the head of this great body, it is called the mother country ; all the fettled inhabitants of this vaft empire are called *Englifhmen,* but individuals, from the place of their nativity or refidence, are called *Englifh, Scotch, Irifh, Welch, Americans, &c.*

Scotland and *Ireland* were originally diftinct kingdoms and nations, but the colonies in *America,* being fettled upon lands difcovered by the *Englifh,* under charters from the crown of *England,* were always confidered as a part of the *Englifh* nation, and of the *Britifh* empire, and looked upon as dependent upon *England*; I mean, that before the union of the two kingdoms, (and very few colonies have been fettled fince) they depended on *England* only, and even now I fuppofe are rather confidered as a dependance upon *England* than of the two kingdoms united under the name of *Great-Britain.* Were it not for the union, which incorporates the two kingdoms, the colonies never would have depended on that part of *Britain* called *Scotland,* and by the terms of the union I apprehend *England* has not given up or brought her colonies under the dominion of *Scotland,* but tho' dependent on *Great-Britain,* they ftill remain what they always were, *Englifh* colonies.

All the inhabitants of the *Britifh* empire together form the BRITISH NATION, and that the *Britifh* Parliament is the fupreme power and legiflature in the *Britifh* nation I never heard doubted.

By the *Englifh* conftitution, which is that which prevails over the whole empire, all *Englifhmen,* or all that make up the *Britifh* empire, are entitled to certain privileges indefeafible, unalienable, and of which they can never be deprived, but by the taking away of that conftitution which gives them thefe privileges. I have obferved that the *Britifh* empire is made up of different kingdoms and nations, but it is not the original conftitution of *Scotland* or *Ireland,* but of *England,* which extends and communicates its privileges to the whole empire. This is an undeniable principle, and ought never to be loft out of fight, if we would form a found judgment on the queftion now to be confidered.

From the confideration above admitted, that the *Britifh* Parliament is the fupreme legiflative power in the whole *Britifh* empire, the following conclufion has been drawn; the colonies (and the fame I fuppofe is meant of all the *Britifh* empire, of which the colonies are a part) are bound by and fubject to all the laws of the *Britifh* Parliament in which they are mentioned, or are fubject to none of any kind whatfoever.

Before

Before this can be properly difcuffed, it muft be obferved, that *Great-Britain* has not only a Parliament, which is the fupreme legif-lature, but alfo a conftitution, and that the now Parliament derives its authority and power trom the conftitution, and not the confti-tution from the Parliament. It may alfo be very fairly inferred hence, that the liberties of *Englifhmen* arife from and depend on the *Englifh* conftitution, which is permanent and ever the fame, where-as the individuals which compofe the Parliament are changed at leaft once every feven years, and always at the demife of a king.

The Parliament of *Great-Britain* is the fupreme legiflature in the *Britifh* empire. It muft be fo either abfolutely or agreeable to the conftitution ; if abfolutely, it can alter the conftitution whenever it fees fit; if abfolutely, it is not bound by the conftitution, nor any thing elfe; if agreeable to the conftitution, then it can no more make laws, which are againft the conftitution, or the unalterable privileges of *Britifh* fubjects, than it can alter the conftitution itfelf. Suppofing a Parliament, under fome of the arbitrary reigns of the laft century, fhould have made a law, that for the future the king's warrant fhould be fufficient to lay a tax on the fubject, or to oblige him to pay fhip money, it would have been an act of the fupreme legiflature, but it may fafely be doubted, whether the nation would have thought it conftitutional. I conclude therefore, that the pow-er of Parliament, and of every branch of it, has its bounds affigned by the conftitution.

If the power of the Parliament is limited by the conftitution, it may not be improper next to enquire, whether the power of the *Britifh* Parliament affects all the fubjects of the *Britifh* empire in the fame manner.

If the power of the *Britifh* Parliament affects all the fubjects of the *Britifh* empire in the fame manner, it follows, that all the laws made by the *Britifh* Parliament are binding alike upon all thofe o-ver whom this power extends, or in other words, that all the fub-jects of the *Britifh* empire are bound not only by thofe laws in which they are exprefsly mentioned, but every law by the Parlia-ment made, for what need is there to mention every individual of thofe for whom the law is made in general, every fubject therefore of the *Britifh* empire, upon this fuppofition, muft be bound by every law of the *Britifh* Parliament, unlefs exprefsly excepted.

Thofe that hold the fubjects of *Great-Britain*, living without *England* or *Scotland*, are bound by every law in which they are men-tioned, feem alfo clearly to hold, that the fame perfons are not bound by fuch laws in which they are not mentioned. Thus the al-ternative, that the fubjects of the *Britifh* empire muft be fubject to all or none of the laws of the *Britifh* Parliament, is limited even by thofe who plead for an univerfal fubmiffion. He that is only bound to obey some laws, cannot be said to be bound by all laws, as, on the contrary, he that is bound to obey all laws, is excused in none.

I suppose, before the union with *Scotland*, none would have scrupled to call the *English* Parliament the supreme legislature of all the *British* empire, though *Scotland* was still an independent kingdom, and by the union *Scotland* and its Parliament was not swallowed up and absorbed by *England* and its Parliament, but united with the kingdom, and the Parliaments also of the two kingdoms united in one general legislature. The ecclesiastical laws and constitution also of each kingdom remains as it was before, *i. e.* entirely different from each other.

Perhaps it may not be amiss to conceive, that the authority of the *British* Parliament extends over the whole *British* nation, though the different respective subjects are not altogether alike affected by its laws: That, with regard to national trade, the power of making it most beneficial to the head and every branch of the empire is vested in the *British* Parliament, as the supreme power in the nation, and that all the *British* subjects every where have a right to be ruled by the known principles of their common constitution.

Next, it may be proper to take a nearer view how far, and in what manner, the acts of Parliament operate upon the different subjects of the *British* empire.

ENGLAND doubtless is the first and primary object of the *British* Parliament, and therefore all laws immediately affect every resident in *England*; and of the king himself it has been said, *Rex Angliæ in regno suo non habet superiorem nisi Deum & legem.* Proceedings at law I take to be the same in *England* and *England*'s dependencies.

SCOTLAND is united with *England*, and therefore there is a different operation of the laws that subsisted before and those that have been made since the union, and even these do not affect *Scotland* as of themselves; but in consequence of and in the terms of the union between the two nations, the union makes no alteration in proceedings at law, nor does it take away any private property.

IRELAND is a distinct kingdom, and hath been conquered from the native *Irish* two or three times by the *English*; it hath nevertheless a Parliament of its own, and is a part of the *British* empire. It will best appear how far the *British* Parliament think *Ireland* dependent upon *Great-Britain*, by inserting, *A Bill for the better securing of the Dependency of* Ireland. The act was as follows: Whereas attempts have lately been made to shake off the subjection of *Ireland* unto, and dependence upon the imperial crown of this realm, which will be of dangerous consequence to *Great-Britain* and *Ireland*. And whereas the House of Lords in *Ireland*, in order thereto, have, of late, against law, assumed to themselves a power and jurisdiction to examine, correct and amend, the judgment and decrees of the courts of justice in the kingdom of *Ireland*; therefore, for the better
ter

ter fecuring of the dependency of *Ireland* upon the crown of *Great-Britain*, may it pleafe your Majefty, that it may be enacted, and it is hereby declared and enacted, by the King's moft excellent Majefty, by and with the advice and confent of the Lords Spiritual and Temporal, and Commons, in this prefent Parliament affembled, and by the authority of the fame, That the faid kingdom of *Ireland* hath been, is, and of right ought to be, fubordinate unto, and dependent upon the imperial crown of *Great-Britain*, as being infeparably united and annexed thereunto, and that the King's Majefty, by and with the advice and confent of the Lords Spiritual and Temporal, and Commons of *Great-Britain*, in Parliament affembled, had, hath, and of right ought to have, full power and authority to make laws and ftatutes of fufficient force and validity to bind the people and kingdom of *Ireland*.

And be it farther enacted, by the authority aforefaid, That the Houfe of Lords of *Ireland* have not, nor of right ought to have, any jurifdiction to judge of, affirm, or reverfe any judgment, fentence, or decree, given or made in any court within the faid kingdom, and that all proceedings before the Houfe of Lords upon any fuch judgment, fentence, or decree, are, and are hereby declared to be utterly null and void to all intents and purpofes whatfoever.

The occafion of this bill was an appeal brought 1719 from the Houfe of Peers in *Ireland* to the Houfe of Peers in *England*. A PITT was the firft that fpoke againft it in the Houfe of Commons, becaufe, as he faid, in his opinion it feemed calculated for no other purpofe than to encreafe the power of the *Britifh* Houfe of Peers, which in his opinion was already but too great. The Duke of *Leeds* protefted againft it in the Houfe of Lords, and gave fifteen reafons to fupport the claim of the Houfe of Peers in *Ireland*. The bill however paffed, though Mr. *Hungerford*, Lord *Molefworth*, Lord *Tyrconel*, and other members, endeavoured to fhew, that *Ireland* was ever independent with refpect to courts of judicature. Some propofals have feveral years ago been made to incorporate *Ireland* with *Great-Britain*, but without any effect.

The Iflands of *Guernfey* and *Jerfey*, though in ecclefiaftical matters confidered as a part of *Hampfhire*, are under the direction of an Affembly call'd the Convention of the States of *Jerfey*, &c. The *Ifle of Man* hath lately been annexed to the crown, but their own *Manks* laws ftill obtain in the ifland.

The *Britifh* colonies and iflands in *America* are not the leaft important part of the *Britifh* empire; that thefe owe a conftitutional dependence to the *Britifh* Parliament I never heard they denied; though of late they have frequently been charged with it, thefe charges have not been grounded upon any declaration of theirs of the kind, their very petitioning, petitions and refolutions, manifeftly

feftly fpeaking the very reverfe; but their averfion to certain new duties, laid upon them for the fole purpofe of raifing a revenue, have been made a handle of againft them, and they have as good as been charged, that they declare themfelves an independent people. Thefe infinuations the *Americans* are apt to look upon as being neither very fair nor very friendly; however at prefent I would only confider what kind of dependence is expected from the *American* colonies. An act of Parliament has fixed that of *Ireland*; a later act of the fame power hath alfo fixed that of *America*, though, as will appear from the comparifon, not altogether on the fame footing. The act is entitled, *An Act for the better fecuring the Dependency of his Majefty's Dominions in* America *upon the Crown and Parliament of* Great-Britain, and runs thus:

Whereas feveral of the Houfes of Reprefentatives in his Majefty's colonies and plantations in *America* have of late, againft law, claimed to themfelves, or to the General Affemblies of the fame, the fole and exclufive right of impofing duties and taxes upon his Majefty's fubjects in the faid colonies and plantations, and, in purfuance of fuch claim, paffed certain votes, refolutions and orders, derogatory to the legiflative authority of Parliament, and inconfiftent with the dependency of the faid colonies and plantations upon the crown of *Great-Britain*, may it therefore pleafe your moft excellent Majefty, that it may be declared, and be it declared, by the King's moft excellent Majefty, by and with the advice and confent of the Lords Spiritual and Temporal, and Commons, in the prefent Parliament affembled, and by the authority of the fame, That the faid colonies and plantations in *America* have been, are, and of right ought to be, fubordinate unto and dependent upon the imperial crown and Parliament of *Great Britain*, and that the King's Majefty, by and with the advice and confent of the Lords Spiritual and Temporal, and Commons, of *Great-Britain*, in Parliament affembled, had, hath, and of right ought to have, full power and authority to make laws and ftatutes of fufficient force and validity to bind the colonies and people of *America*, fubjects of the crown of *Great-Britain*, in all cafes whatfoever.

And be it further declared and enacted, by the authority aforefaid, That all refolutions, votes, orders and proceedings, in any of the faid colonies or plantations, whereby the power and authority of the Parliament of *Great-Britain* to make laws and ftatutes as aforefaid is denied, or drawn into queftion, are, and are hereby declared to be utterly null and void to all intents and purpofes whatfoever.

This is the ftandard of dependence which the Parliament of *Great-Britain* hath fixed for the *Britifh* colonies on the 18th of *March*, 1766. The Stamp Act was repealed the fame day, and the opinion of feveral noblemen who protefted againft that repeal

peal was, " that this declaratory bill cannot poſſibly obviate the
" growing miſchiefs in *America*, where it may ſeem calculated only
" to deceive the people of *Great-Britain*, by holding forth a de-
" luſive and nugatory affirmance of the legiſlative right of *Great-*
" *Britain*, whilſt the enacting part of it does no more than abro-
" gate the reſolutions of the Houſe of Repreſentatives in the
" *North-American* colonies, which have not in themſelves the leaſt
" colour of authority, and declares that which is apparently and
" certainly criminal only null and void." I preſume I may venture to affirm, that in and by this act, the Parliament did not mean
to ſet aſide the conſtitution, infringe the liberties of *Britiſh* ſubjects, or to vindicate unto themſelves an authority which it had
not before, was known to have, and would always have had, though
this act had never been made. I alſo find, that, in order to overſet
any act, law, reſolution, or proceeding, of the colony Aſſemblies,
nothing ſeems neceſſary, but that the Parliament ſhould declare it
null and void to all intents and purpoſes whatſoever. And it ſeems
pretty clear, that the ſame power that can diſannul any act by a
ſimple declaration, with one ſingle ſtroke more, can alſo annihilate
the body that made it.

The remark already made, that though all the different parts
of the *Britiſh* empire are in a ſtate of dependence upon the Parliament of *Great-Britain*, yet that the nature and degree of dependence is not exactly alike in the reſpective different parts of the ſame,
will receive new ſtrength and light, if we compare the act for
better ſecuring the dependency of *Ireland* with that for better ſecuring the dependency of the colonies. Both acts, though at different times, have been made by the ſame authority, and for a ſi-
milar purpoſe, and none can better tell us what kind and degree
of dependency the Parliament expects and requires of its depen-
dents than the Parliament itſelf.

The *Iriſh* is entitled in very general words, for the better ſecuring
the dependency of *Ireland*.

The title of the *American* law is more explicit; *Ireland's* dependency is mentioned, but the dependency of the *Americans* is more
clearly expreſſed, and ſaid to be upon the crown and Parliament of
Great-Britain. *America* ſeems to owe two dependencies, one to the
crown, and one to the Parliament.

The preamble of the *Iriſh* bill brings no leſs a charge than an
attempt to ſhake off ſubjection unto and dependence upon the imperial crown of *Great-Britain*.

The preamble of the *American* bill brings no ſuch accuſation,
but only, that the *Americans* have claimed an excluſive right to lay
on taxes on his Majeſty's ſubjects within the colonies, and paſſed
votes and reſolutions derogatory to the legiſlative power of Parliament, and inconſiſtent with the dependency of the ſaid colonies

C   and

and plantations upon the crown (the word and Parliament is not made ufe of in this place) of *Great-Britain*. The principal differences between thefe bills feems to me to lie in this, that *Ireland* is faid to be fubject to and dependent only on the crown of *Great-Britain*, whereas *America* throughout is declared fubject, at leaft dependent and fubordinate, not only to the crown, but alfo to the Parliament of *Great-Britain*, and then *Ireland* is only declared dependent upon, and fubordinate to, in very gentle terms, whereas the right of making laws to bind the *Americans* is expreffed in thefe very ftrong, moft extenfive terms, IN ALL CASES WHATSOEVER.

Time was when the dependency of the colonies upon *England* was fpoke of exactly in the terms made ufe of for *Ireland*; the charter of this province faith, "our pleafure is, that the tenants and inhabitants of the faid province be fubject IMMEDIATELY to the crown of *England*, as depending thereof forever;" but by the late law all *America* is faid to be dependent on crown and Parliament. This alteration feems to me by no means immaterial, but to imply a change both in the fubjection expected from the colony and in the authority to which the colony owes dependency and fubordination. In Parliament, King, Lords, and Commons, conftitute the fupreme power; but as each of thefe has its own diftinct unalienable right, and incommunicable prerogatives, rights, or privileges, fo I cannot but conceive dependency upon the crown and dependency upon crown and Parliament are things not exactly alike. If (as afferted in the charter) the colonies at fome time or other were only dependent on the crown, and now are fubordinate unto and dependent upon crown and Parliament, it fhould feem both the authority on which they depend, and the nature of their dependency, hath undergone fome alteration; neither doth this appear to me a trifling alteration, and it feems to me at leaft if fo it muft needs make fome alteration in the fyftem of government and obebience.

Hitherto all appeals from the colonies, after paffing thro' chancery in *America*, have been made to the King in council; this I conceive muft have been in confequence of the dependency of the colonies immediately upon the crown; but perhaps for the future appeals will not be carried to the King in council, but to the King and Parliament.

The crown has hitherto had a right of a negative upon all *American* laws, and they were obliged to be paffed in *America* with a faving claufe; but if, as is afferted in the declaratory bill, the King has a right and power to make laws to bind the *Americans*, *by and with the advice and confent of the Lords Spiritual and Temporal and Commons of* Great-Britain, *affembled in Parliament*, then probably the fame authority muft alfo concur to repeal the laws made in *America*, whereas the crown hitherto repealed any law made in A-

merica

merica without asking or waiting for the consent of Lords and Commons.

It appears also, by a late act suspending the Assembly of *New-York*, that the parliamentary authority also extends to suspend, which is but another word for proroguing or dissolving (or annihilating) Assemblies; all which has hitherto been done by the crown without the interfering of Parliament: But that the crown hath a right of proroguing or dissolving the Parliament itself by its own authority I suppose will not be denied. I cannot dismiss this subject without observing, that even the declaratory bill speaks of the Assemblies in *America* as Houses of Representatives. If it is allowed that they are represented in *America*, unless they are represented doubly, they cannot be represented any where else; this strikes at the root of virtual representation, and if representation is the basis of taxation, they cannot be taxed but where they are represented, unless they are doubly taxed, as well as doubly represented.

It is evident upon the whole, that a much greater degree of dependency and subordination is expected of *America* than of *Ireland*, though, by the way, *Ireland*, in the preamble of their bill, is charged with much greater guilt than *America*; nay, the words in ALL CASES WHATSOEVER are so exceeding extensive, that, in process of time, even hewing of wood, and drawing of water, might be argued to be included in them.

It was necessary to state the authority claimed by Parliament over *America* as clear and full as possible; with regard to the *Americans* it must be owned, when they profess to owe dependency and subordination to the *British* Parliament, they do not mean so extensive and absolute a dependency as here seems to be claimed, but that they think themselves in a constitutional manner dependent upon and in subordination to the crown and Parliament of *Great-Britain*, even those votes, resolutions, and proceedings, which are disannulled by the House of Commons and the declaratory bill, most fully and chearfully declare.

It has indeed been said, that unless they are subject to all the *British* acts in which they are mentioned, they are subject to none of any kind whatsoever, and consequently to be considered as independent of the legal and parliamentary power of *Great-Britain*; but I should think it might be as fairly and safely concluded, that while the *Americans* declare themselves subject to any one law of the *British* legislature, it cannot be said they declare themselves independent, or not subject to any law whatever.

In so delicate and important a matter, may I be permitted to observe, that the measure of power and of obedience in every country must be determined by the standard of its constitution. The dispute seems to lie between the Parliament and colonies; the Parliament will certainly be the sitting judges; I will not take upon
me

me to fay that the *Americans* may not look upon Parliament as judge and party; however, it is very poffible for a judge to give a moſt righteous fentence, even where he himfelf is deeply interefted, but they that are fufferers by the fentence will ever be apt to wifh that he had not been party as well as judge.

From what hath been faid hitherto, the due and conftitutional authority of the *Britiſh* Parliament appears clear, and it does not lefs fo I hope, that the fubordination to and dependency on the *Britiſh* Parliament is not exactly the fame in all the refpective parts of that extenfive empire; perhaps this will appear with ftill greater evidence by taking a particular view of the fubject of taxation.

Any unlimited power and authority may lay on the fubjects any tax it pleafeth; the fubjects in that cafe themfelves are mere property, and doubtlefs their fubftance and labour muft be at their difpofal who have the difpofal of their perfons. This is the cafe in arbitrary governments; but the *Britiſh* empire is an empire of freemen, no power is abfolute but that of the laws, and, as hath been afferted, of fuch laws to which they that are bound by them have themfelves confented.

Did the power and authority of the *Britiſh* Parliament in point of taxation extend in the fame manner over all its dependencies, *e. g.* the fame over *Scotland* as over *England*, over *Ireland* in the fame manner as over *Scotland*, over *Guernfey* and *Jerfey* as over *Ireland*, &c. then the very fame act which lays a general tax would lay it alfo at the fame time upon all over whom that authority extends. The laws of every legiflature are fuppofed to extend to and be made over all within their jurifdiction, unlefs they are exprefsly excepted. Thus an excife law extends to all the *Britiſh* kingdom, becaufe it is a publick law; but acts have frequently been made to lay on a penny *Scots* on beer, which, being for a local purpofe, cannot operate on the whole kingdom. The fame I believe may be faid with regard to the method of recovering fmall debts; it feems abfurd to fay, that any fupreme legiflature makes an unlimited law which at the fame time is defigned not to be binding upon the greateft part of the fubjects within that empire. Was it ever known that the land tax being laid on the whole united kingdom, the bifhoprick of *Durham*, and the manor of *Eaſt-Greenwich*, were not alfo fuppofed to be included? and if any part within the immediate jurifdiction, and equally dependent on the fame legiflature, fhould be defigned to be excufed from, or not liable to pay a general tax, would it not be abfolutely neceffary that fuch a place fhould be exprefsly excepted? If, becaufe *America* is a part of the *Britiſh* empire, it is as much fo, or in the fame manner is a part of it, as is the bifhoprick of *Durham*, or the manor of *Eaſt-Greenwich*, nothing can be plainer than that it muft be affected by every tax that is laid juft in the fame manner and proportion as is the bifhoprick of *Durham*, or manor

of

East-Greenwich. This hath not been the case, nor thought to be the case hitherto. *Ireland* and *America* have not been called upon to pay the *British* land tax, malt tax, nor indeed any tax in which they have not been expresly mentioned; the reason of which I presume must be, either that the *British* Parliament did not look upon them as any part of the kingdom of *Great-Britain*, or else did not think them liable to any tax in which they were not expresly mentioned. If any subjects of the *British* empire are not liable to any or every tax laid on by the *British* Parliament, it must be either because they are not liable by the constitution, (as not being reprefented) or because they are excused by the favour of Parliament; if they are not liable by the privileges of the constitution, their not being compelled to pay is no favour, the contrary would be oppression and an anticonstitutional act; if they have been hitherto excused by the lenity of the *British* Parliament, it must be owned the Parliament bore harder on those who were made to pay those taxes than on those who by their lenity only were excused.

The noble Lords who protested against the repeal of the Stamp Act observe, " it appears to us, that a most essential part of that " authority, (*sc.* the whole legislative authority of *Great-Britain*, " without any distinction or referve whatsoever) the power of le- " gistation, cannot be properly, equitably, or impartially exerci- " ed, if it does not extend itself to all the members of the state in " proportion to their respective abilities, but suffers a part to be " exempt from a due share of those burdens which the publick " exigencies require to be imposed upon the whole: A partiality " which is directly and manifestly repugnant to the trust reposed " by the people in every legistature, and destructive of that confi- " dence on which all government is founded."

If in the opinion of these Noblemen, therefore, it is partiality to suffer any part of the state to be exempt from a due share of those burdens which the publick exigencies require should be imposed upon the WHOLE, it would also seem to be a species of partiality, to lay a burden on ANY PART of the state which the other parts of the same state are not equally bound to bear. Partial burdens, or partial exemptions, would doubtless affect those that are burdened or exempted in a very different manner; but if not extending alike to the whole, must still be looked upon as partial. And if this partiality is inconsistent with the trust *reposed BY THE PEOPLE in every legistature*, it would also seem that the legistature could not lay any burdens but as entrusted by the people who chose them to be their representatives and a part of the legistature. We may hence also learn what is to be expected, if every other part of the *British* empire, *England* and *Scotland* only excepted, have hitherto been exempted from the taxes paid in *England*, which it must be owned are very heavy, by mere favour; or, as some seem to express it,

D

It, "*flagrant partiality and injustice*;" their being indulged time immemorial will not be deemed a sufficient plea to excuse them always, but with an impartial hand the very same taxes that now obtain in *Great-Britain* will be laid upon *Ireland, America, Jersey, Guernsey,* the *Mediterranean, African* and *East-India* settlements, and, in short, on every individual part of the *British* empire. Whether a design to do this be not ripening apace I will not take upon me to say, but whenever it does, it must make some alteration in the policy of the mother and infant state, nay in the system of the whole *British* empire.

There are several parts of the *British* empire that pay no tax at all; this I take to be the case of *Gibraltar, Minorca, Newfoundland, East-Florida,* and all the *African* and *East-India* settlements, &c. The reason is, that all these places have no legislature of their own, and consequently none to give or dispose of their property; had these places been taxed by Parliament, there might however this reason been given, that having no representatives within themselves, and having never contributed any thing to the publick burdens, though they all receive protection, perhaps greater than the *American* colonies, the Parliament supplied that defect; but this cannot be urged against the colonies, who both have legislatures, and also contributed to the publick burdens, and that so liberally, that even the crown and Parliament thought they had exerted themselves beyond their abilities, and for several years gave them some compensation. I may mention those parts of the *British* empire as striking instances, that where there is no representation, taxation hath not been thought of, and yet *Newfoundland*, which is not taxed at all, is certainly as much represented in Parliament as all the colonies, which are designed to be doubly taxed.

By the constitution taxes are in the nature of a free gift of the subjects to the crown; regulations of trade are measures to secure and improve the trade of the whole nation. There is no doubt but regulations may be made to ruin as well as to improve trade; yet without regulations trade cannot subsist, but must suffer and sink; and it seems no where more proper to lodge the power of making these regulations than in the highest court of the empire; yet a man may trade or not, he may buy or let it alone; if merchandizes are rated so high that they will not suit him to purchase, though it may be an inconvenience, yet there is no law to compel him to buy; to rate the necessaries of life, without which a man cannot well do, beyond their real value, and hinder him at the same time from purchasing them reasonably of others, is scarce consistent with freedom; but when duties are laid on merchandizes not to regulate trade, but for the express and sole purpose of raising a revenue, they are to all intents and purposes equal to any tax, but they can

by

by no means be called the free gift of thofe who never helped to make the law, but, as far as in them lay, ever looked upon it as an unconftitutional grievance.

If taxes are a free GIFT of the people to the crown, then the crown hath no right to them but what is derived from the GIVERS. It may be abfolutely neceffary that the fubject fhould give, but ftill he that is to give muft be fuppofed the judge both of that neceffity, and how much he may be able and ought to give upon every neceffary occafion. No man can give what is not his own, and therefore the conftitution hath placed this right to judge of the neceffity, and of what is to be given, in the Commons as the reprefentatives of all thofe who are to give, in vefting a right in them to give publick fupplies to the crown; it did not, could not mean to inveft them with any power to give what neither belongs to them, nor thofe whom they reprefent; and therefore, as no man conftitutionally " owes obedience to any law to which he has not affented either in perfon or by his reprefentative;" much lefs doth the conftitution oblige any man to part with his property, but freely and by his own confent; what thofe who are reprefentatives are not willing to give, no power in *Great-Britain* hath any right violently to take, and for a man to have his property took from him under pretence of a law that is not conftitutional, would not be much better than to have it took from him againft the exprefs confent of thofe whom he conftitutionally made his reprefentatives.

It is held a maxim, that in government a proportion ought to be obferved between the fhare in the legiflature and the burden to be borne. The *Americans* pretend to no fhare in the legiflature of *Great-Britain* at all, but they hope they have never forfeited their fhare in the conftitution.

Every government fuppofes rule and protection from the governors, fupport and obedience from thofe that are governed; from thefe duly tempered arifes the prerogative of the crown and the liberty of the fubject; but he that has not a right to his own hath no property, and he that muft part with his property by laws againft his confent, or the confent of the majority of the people, has no liberty. The *Britifh* conftitution is made to fecure liberty and property; whatever takes away thefe takes away the conftitution itfelf, and cannot be conftitutional.

To form a clear judgment on the power of taxation, it muft be enquired on what right that power is grounded. It is a fundamental maxim of *Englifh* law, that there is a contract between the crown and fubjects; if fo, the crown cannot lay on any tax, or any other burden, on the fubject, but agreable to the original contract by authority of Parliament; neither can the Lords properly concur, or the Commons frame a tax bill for any other purpofe but the fup-

port

port of the crown and government, confiftent with the original contract between that and the people.

All fubjects are dependent on and fubordinate to the government under which they live. An *Englifhman* in *France* muft obferve the laws of *France*; but it cannot be faid that the dependency and fubordination in *England* is the fame as dependency and fubordination in *France*. In governments where the will of the fovereign is the fupreme law, the fubjects have nothing to give, their ALL is in the difpofal of the government; there fubjects pay, but having nothing of their own cannot give; but in *England* the Commons GIVE and GRANT. This implies both a free and voluntary act, and that they give nothing but their own property.

Though every part of the *Britifh* empire is bound to fupport and promote the advantage of the whole, it is by no means neceffary that this fhould be done by a tax indifcriminately laid on the whole; it feems fufficient that every part fhould contribute to the fupport of the whole as it may be beft able, and as may beft fuit with the common conftitution.

I have before obferved the different degree of dependency on the mother ftate; I fhall now review the fame again, with a particular regard to impofing or paying taxes, and if a material difference hath always obtained in this refpect, it will confirm my affertion, that every branch of the *Britifh* empire is not affected by the tax laws of *Great-Britain* in the felf fame manner.

The Parliament has a right to tax, but this right is not inherent in the members of it as men; I mean, the members of Parliament are not (like the Senate of *Venice*) fo many rulers who have each of them a native and inherent right to be the rulers of the people of *England*, or even their reprefentatives; they do not meet together as a court of proprietors to confider their common intereft, and agree with one another what tax they will lay on thofe over whom they bear rule, or whom they reprefent, but they only exercife that right which nature hath placed in the people in general, and which, as it cannot conveniently be exercifed by the whole people, THESE have lodged in fome of their body chofen from among themfelves, and by themfelves, for that purpofe, and empowered for a time only to tranfact the affairs of the whole, and to agree in their behalf on fuch fupplies as it may be neceffary to furnifh unto the crown for the fupport of its dignity, and the neceffities and protection of the people.

It would be abfurd to fay, that the crown hath a right to lay on a tax, for as taxes are granted to the crown, fo in this cafe the crown would make a grant to itfelf, and hence the bill of rights exprefsly afferts, that *the levying of money for or to the ufe of the crown, by pretence of prerogative, without grant of Parliament, for a longer time or*

in

[17]

in any other manner than the same is or shall be granted, is illegal; hence also there is a material difference between money bills and all other laws. The King and Lords cannot make any amendment in money bills, as the House of Lords frequently doth in all others, but must accept or refuse them such as they are offered by the Commons, the constitutional reason of which is very obvious, it is the people only that give, and therefore giving must be the sole act of those by whom the givers are represented. The crown cannot take till it is given, and they that give cannot give but on their own behalf, and of those whom they represent; nay even then they cannot give but in a constitutional manner; they cannot give the property of those they represent without giving their own also exactly in the same proportion; every bill must be equally binding upon all whom they represent, and upon every one that is a representative.

Every representative in Parliament is not a representative for the whole nation, but only for the particular place for which he hath been chosen. If any are chosen for a plurality of places, they can make their election only for one of them. The electors of *Middlesex* cannot chuse a representative but for *Middlesex*, and as the right of sitting depends entirely upon the election, it seems clear to demonstration, that no member can represent any but those by whom he hath been elected; if not elected he cannot represent them, and of course not consent to any thing in their behalf. While *Great-Britain*'s representatives do not sit assembled in Parliament, no tax whatever can be laid by any power on *Great-Britain*'s inhabitants; it is plain therefore, that without representation there can be no taxation. If representation arises entirely from the free election of the people, it is plain that the elected are not representatives in their own right, but by virtue of their election; and it is not less so, that the electors cannot confer any right on those whom they elect but what is inherent in themselves; the electors of *London* cannot confer or give any right to their members to lay a tax on *Westminster*, but the election made of them doubtless empowers them to agree to or differ from any measures they think agreeable or disagreeable to their constituents, or the kingdom in general. If the representatives have no right but what they derive from their electors and election, and if the electors have no right to elect any representatives but for themselves, and if the right of sitting in the House of Commons arises only from the election of those designed to be representatives, it is undeniable, that the power of taxation in the House of Commons cannot extend any further than to those who have delegated them for that purpose; and if none of the electors in *England* could give a power to those whom they elected to represent or tax any other part of his Majesty's dominions except themselves, it must follow, that when the Commons are met, they represent no other place or part of his Majesty's dominions, and

E   cannot

cannot give away the property but of thofe who have given them a power fo to do by choofing them their reprefentatives.

The Parliament hath the fole right to lay on taxes, and, as hath been obferved in Parliament, 'tis not the King and Lords that GIVE and GRANT, but this is the fole act of the Commons. The Commons have the right to do fo either from the crown or people, or it is a right inherent in themfelves. It cannot be inherent in themfelves, for they are not born reprefentatives, but are fo by election, and that not for life, but only for a certain time; neither can they derive it from the crown, elfe the liberty and property of the fubject muft be entirely in the difpofal and poffeffion of the crown; but if they hold it entirely from the people, they cannot hold it from any other people but thofe who have chofen them to be their reprefentatives, and it fhould feem they cannot extend their power of taxing beyond the limits of time and place, nor indeed for any other purpofe but that for which they have been chofen. As the Commons in Parliament cannot lay any tax but what they muft pay themfelves, and falls equally on the whole kingdom of *England*, fo, by a fundamental law, they cannot lay but fuch a part of the general tax on fome part of the united kingdom. The principality of *Wales* was never taxed by Parliament till it was incorporated and reprefented, and, poor as it is, it pays now confiderably larger than *Scotland*, which is as big again. When *England* is taxed two millions in the land tax, no more is paid in *Scotland* than 48,000*l*. and yet to lay a higher land tax on *North-Britain* the *British* Parliament cannot, it cannot without breaking the union, that is, a fundamental law of the kingdom. All the right it hath to tax *Scotland* arifes from and muft be executed in the terms of the union.

The Iflands of *Guernfey*, &c. are not taxed by the *British* Parliament at all, they ftill have their own States, and I never heard that the *British* Parliament ever offered to hinder them to lay on their own taxes, or to lay on additional ones, where they are not reprefented.

Ireland

---

* While *Scotland* was yet a feparate kingdom, it was once debated in Parliament, whether a fubfidy fhould firft be granted, or overtures for liberty firft be confidered; when the Queen's Miniftry infifted on the former, a member urged, that it was now plain the nation was to expect no return for their expence and toil, but to be put to the charge of a fubfidy, and to lay down their necks under the yoke of flavery, &c. Another member faid, that he infifted for having a vote upon the queftion which had been put: That he found as the liberties of the nation were fuppreffed, fo the privileges of Parliament were like to be torn from them, but that he would rather venture his life than that it fhou'd be fo, and fhould chufe rather *to die a freeman* than *live a flave*. Some preffed for the vote, adding, that if there was no other way of obtaining fo natural and undeniable a privilege of the Parliament, *they would demand it with their fwords in their hands*. See Annals of Queen *Anne* for 1703, page 76. Thefe were no *American* fpeakers.

Ireland is a conquered kingdom, the greater part of its inhabitants *Papifts*, who in *England* pay double tax. The *Romans* always made a difference between their colonies and their conquefts, and as reafonable, allowed greater and indeed all common liberties to the former. *Ireland* hath been conquered twice again upon the natives fince its firft conqueft, neverthelefs it hitherto had its own legiflature; if the Parliament of *Great-Britain* claims a right to tax them, they never yet have made ufe of that right, and feeing for ages paft they enjoyed the privilege of having their own property difpofed of by reprefentatives in a Parliament of their own, it is very natural to fuppofe, that they think themfelves entitled to thefe things, and the more fo, becaufe, in the very bill that determines their dependency, they are not faid to be dependent on the *Britifh* Parliament, nor yet on crown and Parliament, but only on the crown of *Great-Britain*.

I would now proceed to take a diftinct view of the point in debate between *Great-Britain* and her colonies.

It feems to be a prevailing opinion in *Great-Britain*, that the Parliament hath a right to tax the *Americans*, and that, unlefs they have fo, *America* would be independent of *Great-Britain*.

And it feems to be a prevailing opinion in *America*, that to be taxed without their confent, and where they are not and cannot be reprefented, would deprive them of the rights of *Englifhmen*, nay, in time, with the lofs of the conftitution, would deprive them of liberty and property altogether.

It is eafily feen, that this is a very interefting fubject, the confequences in each cafe very important, though in neither fo alarming and dangerous to *Britain* as to *America*. With regard to *Great-Britain*, if it fhould not prove fo as is claimed, the confequence can only be this, that then no tax can be laid, or revenue be raifed, on the *Americans*, but where they are reprefented, and in a manner which they think confiftent with their natural rights as men, and with their civil and conftitutional liberties as *Britons*. The dependency of *America* upon *Great-Britain* will be as full and firm as ever, and they will chearfully comply with the requifitions of the crown in a conftitutional manner. The queftion is not, whether the *Americans* will withdraw their fubordination, or refufe their affiftance, but, whether they themfelves fhall give their own property, where they are legally reprefented, or, whether the Parliament of *Great-Britain*, which does not reprefent them, fhall take their property, and difpofe of it in the fame manner as they do theirs whom in Parliament they actually reprefent. The *Americans* do not plead for a right to withhold, but freely and chearfully to give. If 100,000*l*. are to be raifed, the queftion is not, fhall they be raifed or no? but fhall the Parliament levy fo much upon the *Americans*, and order

them

them to pay it, as a gift and grant of the Commons of *Great-Britain* to the King? or, shall the *Americans* also have an opportunity to shew their loyalty and readiness to serve the King by freely granting it to the King themselves? It is not to be denied the *Americans* apprehend, that if any power, no matter what the name, where they are not represented, hath a right to lay a tax on them at pleasure, all their liberty and property is at an end, and they are upon a level with the meanest slaves.

England will not lose a shilling in point of property; the rights and privileges of the good people of *Britain* will not be in the least affected, supposing the claim of the *Americans* just and to take place; whereas every thing dreadful appears in view to the *Americans* if it should turn out otherwise. The crown cannot lose; the *Americans* are as willing to comply with every constitutional requisition as the *British* Parliament itself can possibly be. The Parliament cannot lose, it will still have all the power and authority it hitherto had, and ought to have had; and when every branch of the legislature, and every member of the *British* empire, has a true regard to reciprocal duty, prerogative and privilege, the happiness of the whole is best likely to be secured and promoted.

The *Americans* most solemnly disclaim every thought, and the very idea of independency; they are sometimes afraid they are charged with a desire of it, not because this appears to be the real case, but to set their arguments in an invidious light, and to make them appear odious in the sight of their mother country. This is not a dispute about a punctilio, the difference in the consequence is amazingly great; supposing *America* is not taxed where not represented, and supposing things are left upon the same footing in which with manifest advantage to *Britain* and *America* they have been ever since *Britain* had colonies, neither the trade nor authority of *Britain* suffers the least diminution, but the mischief to the colonies is beyond all expression, if the contrary should take place. If they are not to raise their own taxes, all their Assemblies become useless in a moment, all their respective legislatures are annihilated at a stroke; an act passed by persons, most of whom probably never saw, nor cared much for *America*, may destroy all the acts they ever passed, may lay every burden upon them under which they are not expected immediately to sink, and all their civil and religious liberties, for which their forefathers went into this wilderness, and, under the smiles of Heaven, turned it into a garden, and of immense consequence to the mother country, will, or may be at an end at once. Probably the present Parliament or generation would never carry matters to this length, but who knows what might be done in the next? The first settlers of the *American* wilds never expected that would come to pass what we have seen already. It seems as if some evil genius had prevailed of late; had these new

dutie;

duties been laid on payable in *England*, at least the expence of a Board of Commissioners, and of the swarm of new officers, might have been prevented; but it looks as though some men wished that *America* might not only be borne hard upon, but also be made to know and feel that their liberty and property lay at the mercy of others, and that they must not flatter themselves to enjoy them any longer than the good pleasure of some who would willingly take away what they never did give. I have endeavoured candidly to state the question, let us now endeavour to view the claim made on each side as calmly and impartially as possible.

'Tis said the *British* Parliament hath a right to tax the *Americans*. If this proposition is incontrovertible, it must certainly be built on such a basis and such clear principles as will be sufficient to dispose loyal and reasonable men chearfully to acquiesce in it. There are some points in government which perhaps are best never touched upon, but when any question once becomes the subject of publick debate, strength of reason is the sole authority that with men of reason can determine the matter.

If the Parliament of *Great-Britain* have a right to tax the *Americans*, it must either be the same right in virtue of which they have a right to tax *Great-Britain*, and be vested in them by the same power, or it must be a distinct right either inherent in themselves, or vested in them by some other power.

The right of the Commons of *Great-Britain* to lay on taxes arises, as I conceive, from their having been chosen by the people who are to pay these taxes to act in their behalf and as their representatives. There may be other qualifications necessary, that a man be a *Briton* born, subject of the King, possessed of a certain estate, &c. but none is so absolutely necessary as election. He that hath been a representative had a right to refuse or concur in any tax bill whilst a member, but if he is not chosen again in a following Parliament, he hath no right whatever to meddle in the matter; this proves that the power is originally in the people, and the legislative capacity of the whole House, and of every member, depends upon their free election, and is of force no longer than for the time for which they have been elected; this being elapsed, the trust reposed in them entirely ceases, it absolutely returns to the body of the people; in that interval during which the people are unrepresented, any power their representatives might have is entirely and solely in the people themselves, no tax can be laid on, nor any law to bind the people be formed, for this plain reason, because there are no persons qualified for that purpose. The people have not representatives assigned, but chuse them, and being so chosen, the rights of the people reside now in them, and they may, but not before, act in their behalf. Now, when the crown issues writs of election, it is not to

F

empower

empower the electors to chuse representatives for *America*, nor yet for all *Great-Britain*, but only for some certain place specified in the writ; and when the electors of *Great-Britain* chuse representatives, their meaning also is not to chuse representatives for their fellow subjects in *America*, or any where else, but for themselves. In *Great-Britain English* electors cannot elect in behalf of *Scotland*, and *Scotch* electors cannot in behalf of *England*; and for the same reason neither *Scotch* nor *English* can elect any for *America*. These electors do not represent the *Americans*, nor are they their proxies to vote in members in their behalf; neither can *British* electors give any instructions to *British* representatives, or invest them with any power to dispose of the rights and property of any of their fellow subjects without the kingdom of *Great-Britain*. It seems not unreasonable then to conclude, that the right which the elected acquire by their election to pass tax laws binding upon their electors does not at the same time give them a right to represent and lay on taxes on those who never invested them with any such power, and by whom they neither were nor could be elected. If the *Americans* themselves are not received as voters in the bishoprick of *Durham*, manor of *East-Greenwich*, or any place mentioned in their charters, and the same liberty and privileges with those places therein secured unto them, if they are not allowed to chuse any representatives for themselves in the House of Commons, it seems natural, that what they have no right to do themselves, none can have a right to do for them, and so no body can chuse or send a representative for them to any place where they are not allowed to sit or be represented. If so, the electors of *Great-Britain* never in fact elected representatives for *America*, nor could these electors possibly convey any power to give away property where they have no property themselves. The electors do not represent *America*, neither their representatives by them elected; the electors cannot dispose of the property of *America*, therefore they cannot give a power so to do unto others. In *England* there can be no taxation without representation, and no representation without election; but it is undeniable that the representatives of *Great-Britain* are not elected by nor for the *Americans*, and therefore cannot represent them; and so, if the Parliament of *Great Britain* has a right to tax *America*, that right cannot possibly be grounded on the consideration that the people of *Great-Britain* have chosen them their representatives, without which choice they would be no Parliament at all.

If the Parliament of *Great-Britain* has a right to tax the *Americans* distinct from the right which they derive from their electors, and which they exercise as the representatives of the people of *Great-Britain*, then this right they must hold either from the crown, or from the *Americans*, or else it must be a native inherent right in them.

themfelves, at leaft a confequence of their being reprefentatives of the people of *Great-Britain*.

It is plain that the colonies have been fettled by authority and under the fanction of the crown, but as the crown did not referve unto itfelf a right to rule over them without their own Affemblies, but on the contrary eftablifhed legiflatures among them, as it did not referve a right to lay taxes on them in a manner which, were the experiment made in *England*, might be thought unconftitutional, fo neither do I find that a referve of that kind was made by the crown in favour of the Parliament, on the contrary, by the charters all the inhabitants were promifed the enjoyment of the fame and all privileges of his Majefty's liege fubjects in *England*, of which doubtlefs not to be taxed where they are not reprefented is one of the principal. As to any right that might accrue to Parliament from any act or furrender of the *Americans*, I believe it hath never been thought of; they have a profound veneration for the *Britifh* Parliament, they look upon it as the great palladium of the *Britifh* liberties, but ftill they are not there reprefented, they have had their own legiflatures and reprefentatives for ages paft, and as a body cannot be more than in one place at once, they think they cannot be legally reprefented in more than one legiflative body, but alfo think, that by the laws of *England Proteftants* ought not to be doubly taxed, or, what they think worfe, taxed in two places.

If therefore this right of taxing the *Americans* refides in the Commons of *Great-Britain* at all, it muft be an inherent right in themfelves, or at leaft in confequence of their being reprefentatives of the people of *Great-Britain*. The act for better fecuring the dependency of the colonies, which I have inferted at large, evidently feems to tend this way. That the colonies were thought at the difpofal of Parliament one might be led to think, becaufe by that act, from the fimple authority of the crown, which they were till then fubject to by their charters, they were now declared to be fubordinate to and dependent (on the joint authority) of crown and Parliament. Yet, concerning this act, I would only obferve, that however it may determine the cafe from that day, it cannot be the ground on which the fubordination of the colonies originally WAS or now can be built; for it declares not only, that the colonies ARE AND OUGHT TO BE, but alfo that they ALWAYS HAVE BEEN, fubject to crown and Parliament. A law binds after it is made, it cannot bind before it exifts, and fo furely it cannot be faid, that the colonies have *always* been bound by a law which is above a hundred years pofterior to them in point of exiftence. It is alfo a little difficult to reconcile this law with prior charters; our *Carolina* charter makes our province fubject immediately to the crown, and near a hundred years after a law is made to declare, that this was

not

but and must not be the case, but that the *Americans* always were and ought to be subject to crown and Parliament. Perhaps this hath not been so seriously considered as it may hereafter, but neither this nor any law can be supposed to be binding *ex post facto*, or contrary to our fundamental constitution. *Montesquieu* observes, that the *British* constitution (which God preserve) will be lost, whenever the legislative power shall be more corrupted than the executive part of the legislature.

And after all, in this very law, the *Americans* are allowed to be represented in their own Assemblies, and to lay on duties and taxes, though not exclusively; but whether *America*, or any part of the *British* empire, should be liable to have taxes imposed on them by different legislatures, and whether these would not frequently clash with one another to the detriment of crown and subjects, I leave others duly to consider.

It is said, if *America* cannot be taxed by the *British* Parliament, then it would be independent of *Great-Britain*. This is now a very popular cry, and it is well if many join in it only because they know no better. This is not, will not, cannot be the case. *America* confessedly hath not been thus taxed since it was settled; but no body in *Britain* or *America* ever dreamed that *America* was independent. In *England* the people cannot be taxed when the Parliament does not sit, or when it is dissolved; are they then therefore independent. *Scotland* cannot be taxed in the same degree as *England*; is it therefore independent? *Ireland* and *Jersey* have their own legislatures, and so tax themselves; will you call them independent? All those parts of the *British* empire that have no Assemblies pay no taxes at all, neither among themselves, nor to *Great-Britain*; but it will not therefore be said, that they are independent. The Parliament itself claims a right to refuse supplies till their grievances are heard and redressed, this is looked upon as a constitutional remedy against any encroachments by the crown, and hath very often been made use of in former reigns, and yet the Parliament neither claimed nor were charged with a desire of independency. Those who so freely charge with a desire of independency, and even treason and rebellion, would do well to consider, that this charge, heinous as it is, reflects greater disgrace on those who unjustly make it, than on those on whom it is unjustly made. A man of honour would not easily forgive himself whenever he should discover that he made so rash a charge against two millions of people, as innocent, loyal, and well affected to their King and country, as any of his fellow subjects or himself possibly can be. There never was an *American Jacobite*, the very air of *America* is death to such monsters, never any grew there, and if any are transported, or import themselves, loss of speech always attends them. The loyalty of the *Americans* to their King hath not only been ever untainted, it hath never been as much as suspected. There is a difference between independency and uneasiness. In the late reign, the people in *England* were uneasy at the *Jew* Bill, and it was rapidly repealed; in the present, the Cyder Act was an odious measure, and immediately altered, and that without any disgrace or diminution of parliamentary authority. If there hath been any appearance of riot in *America*, perhaps it may hereafter appear at whose instigation, the law was ever open, and even overbearing odious Custom-House Officers might have been redressed, if they had thought fit to apply for a legal rather than a military remedy. In *England* it is possible Majesty itself hath met with indignities which have not been shewn in *America* even to those men to whom the nation in general is indebted for the present uneasiness, and it is not improbable, that, after all that hath been said and done, the *Americans* will be found an exception to the general rule, that oppression makes even a wise man mad: An ancient rule, the truth of which hath been experienced in *England* oftener than in *America*. The opinion of the *Americans* is, that to be taxed where they are not represented would deprive them of the rights of *Englishmen*, nay, in time, with the loss of the constitution, might and must deprive them of liberty and property altogether. These it must be owned are gloomy apprehensions; two millions of people are so thoroughly prepossessed with them, that even their children unborn may feel the parents impressions; should there be any real ground for them, the *Americans* can hardly be blamed; they sit uneasy under them; they can no more help their uneasiness, than deny the blood which glows in their veins, or be angry with the milk that was their first nourishment. This is not a dark abstruse point, but seems plain and essenttial to the very being of liberty. The sole question is, Is it, or is it not, the right of an *Englishman* not to be taxed where he is not represented? Can you be tired of being represented, O *Britons*! Is it consistent with the constitution you so justly boast of to be thus taxed? Then representation is not essential to your constitution, and sooner or later you will either give it up or be deprived of it. A borough that does not exist shall send two representatives, a single county, neither the largest nor richest, shall send forty-four members, and two millions of souls, and an extent of land of eighteen hundred miles in length, shall have taxes laid on them by such as never were nearer to them than one thousand leagues, and whose interest it may be to lay heavy burdens on them in order to lighten their own. And are these, who are thus taxed, unrepresented, unheard and unknown, *Englishmen*, and taxed by *Englishmen*? Do these enjoy what the charters most solemnly ensure them, the same

G   and all the privileges of the subjects born and resident within the realm? I must doubt it.

Let those who make light of *American* grievances give a plain answer to this plain question, Are the colonies to be taxed by Parliament represented in Parliament? if they are, by whom, or since when? if not, once more, Is it, or is it not, the right of *Britons* not to be taxed where not represented? Here the whole matter hinges, and surely the question is not so impertinent but a civil answer might be given before a mother sends fire and sword into her own bowels. When constitutional liberty is once lost, the transit is very short to the loss of property; the same power that may deprive of the one may also deprive of the other, and with equal justice, those that have not liberty enough to keep their property in reality have no property to keep. Some that look no further build right upon power, and insist the Parliament can do so. If power is all that is meant very like it may, so it may alter the constitution. If a stately tree should take umbrage at some diminutive shrubs, it can fall upon and crush them, but it cannot fall upon them without tearing up its own roots; it can crush those within reach, but its own branches will take off the weight of the impression, permit the shrubs to send forth new shoots, while there is no great probability that the envious oak will return to its former stand and vigour. *Ce'st une chose a bien considerer*, (this ought to be well considered first) said *Moliere's Malade imaginaire*, when his quack proposed to him to have one of his arms cut off, because it took some of the nourishment which in that case would center in the other, and make it so much the stronger. If every Assembly in *America* is suspended, the consequence must be, that the people are without their usual legislature, and in that case nothing short of a miracle seems capable to prevent an anarchy and general confusion. No power can alter the nature of things, that which is wrong cannot be right, and oppression will never be productive of the love and smiles of those that feel it.

The Parliament can crush the *Americans*, but it can also, and with infinitely greater certainty and ease, conciliate their affections, have the ultimate gain of all their labours, and by only continuing them the privileges of *Britons*, that is, by only doing as they would be done by, diffuse the blessings of love and concord throughout the whole empire, and to the latest posterity; and which of these two is the most eligible, it is NOW for you, O *Britons!* to consider, and in considering it, *majores vestros cogitate & posteros*, think on your ancestors and your posterity.

Those whom God hath joined together, (Great-Britain and America, Liberty and Loyalty) let no man put asunder: And may peace and prosperity ever attend this happy union.   FEB. 1, 1769.

THE LAW OF *LIBERTY*.

A SERMON

ON

AMERICAN AFFAIRS,

PREACHED

AT THE OPENING OF THE PROVINCIAL CONGRESS OF *GEORGIA*.

ADDRESSED

TO THE RIGHT HONOURABLE
THE EARL OF *DARTMOUTH*.

WITH AN APPENDIX,

GIVING A CONCISE ACCOUNT OF THE STRUGGLES OF SWISSERLAND TO RECOVER THEIR LIBERTY.

BY JOHN J. ZUBLY, *D. D.*

S. XI: 13. EPHRAIM SHALL NOT ENVY JUDAH, AND JUDAH SHALL NOT VEX EPHRAIM.

PHILADELPHIA:
PRINTED BY HENRY MILLER. MDCCLXXV.

To the RIGHT HONOURABLE

WILLIAM HENRY,

EARL of DARTMOUTH.

MY LORD,

YOUR Lordſhip's appointment to be Se-
cretary of State for the American depart-
ment, by numbers that reſpected your Lordſhip's
religious character, was looked upon as a very
providential and happy event. Your patronizing
of religious undertakings, confirmed the general
opinion, and we were happy in the expectations
of your Lordſhip's conſcientious regard to juſtice
and equity, as well as to the civil and religious
liberties of this great Continent; we expected the
cauſe of liberty and religion would meet with the
ſtrongeſt ſupport under your adminiſtration, and
in your Lordſhip would ever find a conſtant and
ſuccefsful advocate with your royal maſter.

A 2   Unhap-

Unhappily during your adminiſtration, meaſures have been purſued very contrary to American hopes, and we eaſily conceive your Lordſhip may think it not leſs ſtrange that many
friends of religion in America ſhould be ſo un-
eaſy under laws which had your Lordſhip's con-
currence and approbation.

It is to the Man and to the Chriſtian I wiſh
to be permitted to addreſs myſelf : Your Lordſhip ranks among the higheſt ſubjects, and has a
large ſhare in all public meaſures, but anxiety
for what may diſtreſs, and zeal for the welfare
of the empire, can be no crime even in the
meaneſt; and when a houſe is once in flames,
every man is inexcuſable, or muſt at leaſt be ſo
in his own breaſt, that does not contribute whatever he may think in his power to their being
extinguiſhed. The effects of the preſent meaſures
are viſible, and it requires no ſagacity to foreſee
what may be the conſequence, ſhould they be
continued. Your Lordſhip may do much towards reſtoring and perpetuating the tranquility
of a great empire; perſons of my ſtation have
nothing to offer but hints and wiſhes, ſhould
theſe be beneath your notice, or ſtand in need
of forgiveneſs, my ſincere wiſh to contribute any
thing

thing towards a juft, happy and perpetual connexion between a parent ftate and an infant
country growing apace to the moft aftonifhing
importance, muft be my only apology. *Pulchrum
eft bene facere reipublicæ, fed & bene dicere non eft
abfurdum.*

The queftion, My Lord, which now agitates
Great-Britain and America, and in which your
Lordfhip has taken fuch an active part, is,
whether the Parliament of Great-Britain has a
right to lay taxes on the Americans, who are
not, and cannot, there be reprefented, and
whether the Parliament has a right to bind the
Americans in all cafes whatfoever? Whatever
may be faid, or whatever the good people in
Great-Britain may believe, this is the whole
fubject of the difpute. All the feverities hitherto exercifed upon the Americans profeffedly have
no other view than to enforce fuch a dependance,
and nothing lefs than a claim deftructive of all
natural and national liberty, could poffibly have
united all America in a general oppofition, or
have aroufed them to join all like one man in
their common defence. Let a declaratory bill be
paffed, that any law and ufage to the contrary
notwithftanding, America is entitled to all the

common

common rights of mankind and all the bleffings of the Britifh conftitution, that the fword fhall never be drawn to abridge, but to confirm, her birthright, and the ftorm inftantly becomes a calm, and every American thinks himfelf happy to contribute to the neceffities, defence and glory of Great-Britain to the utmoft of his ftrength and power.

To bind them in ALL CASES WHATSOEVER, my Lord, the Americans look upon this as the language of defpotifm in its utmoft perfection. What can, fay they, an Emperor of Morocco pretend more of his flaves than to bind them in all cafes whatfoever. Were it meant to make the Americans hewers of wood and drawers of water, were it meant to oblige them to make bricks without ftraw, were it meant to deprive them of the enjoyment of their religion, and to eftablifh a hierarchy over them fimilar to that of the church of Rome in Canada? it would, fay they, be no more than a natural confequence of the right of binding them (unfeen, unheard, unreprefented) in all cafes whatfoever.

My Lord, the Americans are no ideots, and they appear determined not to be flaves. Oppreffion

preffion will make wife men mad, but oppreffors
in the end frequently find that they were not
wife men : there may be refources even in defpair
fufficient to render any fet of men ftrong enough
not to be bound in all cafes whatfoever.

Grievous is the thought, my Lord, that a nobleman of your Lordfhip's character fhould be fo
zealous to make war, and to imbrue his hands in
the blood of millions of your fellow-fubjects and
fellow-chriftians: Pray, my Lord, is it poffible
that thofe, who at three thoufand miles diftance
can be bound in all cafes, may be faid to have any
liberty at all? Is it nothing in your Lordfhip's
eye to deprive fo confiderable a part of the globe
of the privilege of breathing a free air, or to fub-
jugate numbers and generations to flavery and
defpotifm? Can your Lordfhip think on thefe
things without horror, or hope they muft be
productive of any thing but deteftation and dif-
appointment? Your Lordfhip believes a Supreme
Ruler of the earth, and that the fmall and great
muft ftand before him at laft: Would your
Lordfhip be willing, at the general meeting of
all mankind, to take a place among thofe who
deftroyed or enflaved empires, or rifk you- future
ftate on the merit of having, at the expent. of

Britifh

Britifh blood and treafure, taken away the property, the life and liberty of the largeft part of
the Brittifh empire? Can your Lordfhip think
thofe that fear the LORD will not cry to him
againft their oppreffors, and will not the Father
of mankind hear the cries of the oppreffed? or
would you be willing that their cries and tears
fhould rife againft you as a forward inftrument
of their oppreffion.

I know, my Lord, that this is not courtly
language, but your Lordfhip is a profeffor of religion, and of the pure, gentle, benevolent religion of JESUS CHRIST: The groans of a people
pufhed on a precipice, and driven on the very
brink of defpair, will prove forcible, till it can
be proved that any power, in whofe legiflation
the Americans have no part, may at pleafure
bind them in all cafes whatfoever; till it
can be proved that fuch a claim does not conftitute the very effence of flavery and defpotifm;
till it can be proved that the Americans (whom
in this view I can no longer call Britons) may,
and of right ought, to be thus bound; abhorrence of fuch affertions is only the language of
truth, which in the end will force its way, and
rife

rise superior to all the arts of falshood and all the powers of oppression.

Right or wrong, my Lord, in all cases whatsoever, but more especially when the fate of nations is concerned, are words of infinite moment. Your Lordship doubtless believes that the weighty alternative must have very solemn and different effects here and hereafter; but waving the right or wrong of this vile unhappy dispute, let me entreat your Lordship's attention to consider at what an infinite risk the present measures must be pursued, even were it not demonstrable that they are in the highest degree wrong, cruel and oppressive.

The bulk of the inhabitants of a continent extending eighteen hundred miles in front on the atlantic, and permitting an extension in breadth as far as the south sea, look upon the claim, to bind them in all cases whatsoever, as unjust, illegal and detestable, let us suppose for a moment that they are grosly mistaken; yet an error imbibed by millions, and in which they believe the ALL of the present and future generations lies at stake, may prove a very dangerous error; destroying the Americans will not cure

B   them,

them, nor will any acts that condemn to ftarve or be miferable, have any tendency to perfuade them that thefe acts were made by their friends. The people in England are made to believe that the Americans want to feparate from them, or are unwilling to bear their part of the common burden. No reprefentation can be more falfe; but, my Lord, a nation cannot be mifled always, and when once the good people of Great-Britain get truer notions of the matter, they will naturally wreak their refentment on thofe by whom they have been grofsly mifinformed or wretchedly deceived.

Review, my Lord, the effects of the prefent meafures; the paft and prefent will inform your Lordfhip of what may be to come.

With an unparalleled patience did the Boftonians bear the annihilation of their trade, the blocking up of their harbour, and many other diftreffes, till at Lexington an attack was made upon their lives, and then they gave fufficient proof that their patience was not the effect of timidity, but of prudence and an unwillingnefs to fhed Britifh blood. This attack convinced all America that the Britifh miniftry and troops

were

were athirst after their blood, and the behaviour of both parties on that day, and in many little skirmishes since, must convince all the world that in the cause of liberty the Americans are not afraid to look regulars in the face, and that in an unjust and oppressive service British troops are far from being invincible.

The burning of the innocent town of Charlestown, after it had been left by its inhabitants, is a piece of such wanton cruelty as will fix an everlasting disgrace on the British arms. In the long civil war in Great-Britain nothing of the kind was attempted by either party, and this barbarity cannot fail being condemned by all civilized nations.

If at the battle on Bunker's hill the Americans have been surprized, superiority has cost the regulars' dearer than the Americans what is called their defeat, one or two more such defeats of the Americans would forever put it out of the power of the present regular army to gain a victory.

The rejecting of the New-York petition has

effectually

effectually filenced all thofe who pleaded for, or
hoped any good from, petitioning. The can-
nonading of that town in the dead of the night,
and without the leaft previous warning, as it has
fhewn what the inhabitants are indifcriminately
to expect, will in hiftory ftand as a lafting mo-
nument of fuch wantonnefs of cruelty as nations
not remarkable for humanity would be afhamed
of.

The deftroying of the New-England fifhery
laid all thofe who were deprived of their bread
and occupation at fea, under an abfolute neceffity of feeking it in the American army, and the
fenfe of the injury done them will doubtlefs
exert itfelf in the day of battle.

The endeavour to ftir up popifh Canadians
and favage Indians againft the Colonifts has been
productive of the taking of the important pafs
of Ticonderoga, which has been effected without the lofs of a fingle life on either fide.

Detaining the inhabitants of Bofton, after
they had, in dependance on the General's word
of honour, given up their arms, to be ftarved
and

and ruined, is an action worthy of the caufe, and can only be equaled by the diftreffes of Proteftants driven under the walls of Londonderry, at which even a James relented.

Propofals publicly made by minifterial writers relative to American domeftics, laid the fouthern provinces under a neceffity of arming themfelves; a propofal to put it in the power of domeftics to cut the throats of their mafters, can only ferve to cover the propofers and abettors with everlafting infamy.

The Americans have been called " a rope of " fand;" but blood and fand will make a firm cementation, and enough American blood has been already fhed to cement them together into a thirteenfold cord, not eafily to be broken.

My Lord, the violence of the prefent meafures has almoft inftantaneoufly created a continental union, a continental currency, a continental army, and before this can reach your Lordfhip, they will be as equal in difcipline as they are fuperior in caufe and fpirit to any regulars. The moft zealous Americans could not
have

have effected in an age, what the cruelty and violence of adminiftration has effectually brought to pafs in a day.

The regular army employed on this errand, with four able generals, now lies no better than befieged within the ruins of Charlestown and Bofton, unable to procure the neceffaries of life, obliged to import their bread from Europe, and fuel from Canada, pining away with difeafe, and affording daily martyrs to cruelty and arbitrary power, while every day adds to the improbability of their ever obtaining thofe unhappy ends. A ftrange fituation for a Britifh army!

Reftraining the trade of the Colonies, will effectually annihilate all their trade with Great-Britain. The numbers that croffed the atlantic, or re-exported American commodities from Great-Britain, the manufacturers that wrought for America, or worked up her raw materials, will now be at full leifure to know and feel whether the American trade be an object of any importance, and how much the nation is obliged to a miniftry that has fo effectually laboured its deftruction.

The

The prefent difpute has made every American acquainted with, and attentive to, the principles of the Brittifh conftitution: In this refpect, as well as in a ftrong fenfe of liberty, and
the ufe of fire-arms almoft from the cradle, the
Americans have vaftly the advantage over men of
their rank almoft every where elfe. From the conftant topic of prefent converfation, every child
unborn will be impreffed with the notion: It is
flavery to be bound at the will of another in all
cafes whatfoever; every mother's milk will convey
a deteftation of this maxim. Were your Lordfhip
in America, you might fee little ones acquainted
with the word of command before they can diftinctly fpeak, and fhouldering the refemblance
of a gun before they are well able to walk.

When millions of free people at once turn
their thoughts from trade, and the means of ac-
quiring wealth, to agriculture and frugality, it
muft caufe a moft fenfible alteration in the ftate.
My Lord, this is the cafe at prefent in America;
every new act of violence will ftrengthen and
confirm the fpirit that taught them the neceffity
of being frugal and virtuous, that they might
remain free, and become invincible.

Admit,

Admit, my Lord, (for fuppofitions now become probable in proportion of their being aftonifhing and violent) that a Brittifh fleet may effectually guard every harbour, river, creek or inlet on the American coaft; admit alfo that her troops deftroy every town, village or hut along the feafhore, what then will be the confequence? Why, my Lord, it will be the deftroying the property of thoufands in Great-Britain, and of a few on this fide of the water, whom your Lordfhip calls your friends; perhaps the attempt may not fucceed, but fuppofing it fhould, the Americans, injured beyond a poffibility of reparation, and irritated to the higheft degree, will retire where they are inacceffible to troops and fhips; inftead of trade and navigation, you will have a defolate fea-coaft, the trade of America will be loft, and with it the finews of war: And, my Lord, in the natural courfe of things America, in lefs than half a century, will contain more inhabitants than Great-Britain and Ireland; and that period, my Lord, is not fo far diftant, to put the prefent treatment entirely out of remembrance. America and Great-Britain joined in arms together, may grow confident againft the world befides; but if Britain continue her

arms

arms againſt America; if her troops can be per-
ſuaded to go on againſt their brethren and friends,
if they will deſtroy the laſt aſylum of liberty,
and a country which has ſaved ſo many thouſands from ſtarving at home, the Americans will
fight like men, who have every thing at ſtake;
the mercenaries with bayonets at their backs,
and at the rate of ſix-pence a day; if they are
once defeated, whence will they be reſupplied;
if they return to Britain victorious, they will be
fit inſtruments to promote that ſlavery at home
which they have been ſuccefsful in faſtening
(probably for a very little while) on their fellow-
ſubjects abroad.

In times of public confuſion men of all parties are ſometimes carried further than they intended at firſt ſetting out. Hiſtory and the knowledge of human nature ſhould inform your Lordſhip how much it is againſt all ſound policy to
ſecure or ſtrive for punctilios at an infinite riſk.

The Americans have always ſhewn an affectionate regard to the king, and they are truly
ſenſible of the neceſſity and advantage of a perpetual union with the parent ſtate; but unde-

ſerved

served severities cannot be productive of any
Ⅎasing returns. The Americans firmly believe
that the claim at present endeavouring to be en-
forced, would render them mere slaves, and it is
their general motto, "DEATH OR FREEDOM."
The parliamentary, or, as they say, ministerial,
claim is now written in letters of blood, and
that will be far from making it more acceptable
to American readers.

On the whole, my Lord, should this address
be deemed impertinent and intrusive, I hope it
may still be excusable from the importance of
the cause, and the sincerity of its motive. In the
event of the present dispute I look upon all mankind as interested, and though not natural born,
his Majesty has not another subject that more
ardently wisheth that his own repose and happiness and that of all his subjects may never meet
with any interruption. Whether British troops
shall now drive liberty from out of the greater
part of the British empire, and bury her remains
in the American wilderness, or whether that
wilderness shall flourish and chearfully contribute
to make Great-Britain the greatest empire of the
universe, is the question now to be decided, and
it

it is not fo unimportant, but it may be expected
HE that is higher than the higheft, and taketh up
the ifles like a very little thing, will interpofe in
the decifion. The whole American procefs, my
Lord, is liable to a revifion, and when righteoufnefs and judgment to come once make an im-
preffion, many a Felix will tremble.

To reftore peace and harmony nothing is neceffary than to fecure to America the known
bleffings of the Brittifh conftitution. This may
be done in a moment, and without any difgrace
or rifk. Let the Americans enjoy, as hitherto,
the privilege to GIVE and GRANT by their own
reprefentatives, and they will give and grant liberally; but their liberty they will never part
with but with their lives. The day that reftores
their liberty, reftores every thing to the former
channel; to enforce the contrary claim, ages
may be infufficient, and every day encreafes the
danger of " a mother's being dafhed to pieces
" on her own children."

That your Lordfhip, in the hand of Providence, may be a happy inftrument to bring the
prefent unnatural conteft to a fpeedy, juft and

C 2

honour-

honourable iffue; that you may live to fee much of that happinefs which muft be the refult; is no lefs my fervent prayer, than that God would blaft every counfel and meafure that may have a contrary tendency,——that would feparate Britain and America, whom God has joined together,——that would abridge the rights, liberties and happinefs of the nation, our rightful Sovereign (whom God ever preferve), or any of his fubjects.

I am, my Lord,

Your LORDSHIP's

moft humble fervant,

September 3, 1775.

J. J. ZUBLY.

A SERMON, &c.

JAMES ii: 12.

So speak ye, and so do, as they that shall be judged by the Law of Liberty.

THERE was a time when there was no king in Israel, and every man did what was good in his own eyes. The consequence was a civil war in the nation, issuing in the ruin of one of the tribes, and a considerable loss to all the rest.

And there was a time when there was a king in Israel, and he also did what was right in his own eyes, a foolish son of a wise father; his own imprudence, the rashness of his young counsellors, his unwillingness to redress the grievances of the nation, and the harsh treatment he gave to those who applied for relief, also brought on a civil war, and issued in the separation of the ten tribes from the house of David. He sent his treasurer to gather an odious duty or tribute, but the children of Israel stoned him that he died; and when he gathered one hundred and four score thousand men, that he might bring again the kingdom unto Roboam, GOD sent them a message, " ye shall not go up, nor fight against your brethren, return every man to his house, for this thing is done of me " GOD disapproved of the oppressive measures and ministry of Roboam, and that

king's

king's army appears more ready to obey the command of their GOD, than slay their brethren by orders of a tyrant. " They obeyed the voice of the LORD, and " returned from going against Jeroboam." 2 Chron. x : 18. xi : 4.

The things that happened before are written for our learning. By comparing past times and proceedings with these that are present, prudence will point out many salutary and religious leffons. The conduct of Roboam verifies the lamentation of his father, " Woe to thee, o land, when thy king is a child." Ecclef. x : 16. A very fmall degree of juftice and moderation might have preferved his kingdom, but he thought weapons of war better than wifdom; he hearkened not, neither to the people, nor to fome of his more faithful counfellors, and the confequence was that, inftead of enflaving the ten tribes who ftood up for their liberty, GOD gave Judah to be fervants to the king of Egypt, that they might learn the difference between his fervice and the fervice of the kingdoms of the nations. A people that claim no more than their natural rights, in fo doing, do nothing difpleafing unto GOD; and the moft powerful monarch that would deprive his fubjects of the liberties of man, whatever may be his fuccefs, he muft not expect the approbation of GOD, and in due time will be the abhorrence of all men.

In a time of public and general uneafinefs it behoves both fuperiors and inferiors to confider. It is eafy to extinguifh a fpark, it is folly to blow up difcontent into a blaze; the beginning of ftrife is like the letting out of waters, and no man may know where it will end. There is a rule given to magiftrates and fubjects; which, if carefully attended to, would fecure the dignity and fafety of both; which, if not duly regarded, is ufually

attended

attended with the worst consequences. The present, my hearers, will easily be allowed is a day of trouble, and surely in this day of adversity we ought to consider. When a people think themselves oppressed, and in danger, nothing can be more natural than that they should enquire into the real state of things, trace their grievances to their source, and endeavour to apply the remedies which are most likely to procure relief: This I take to be the design of the present meeting of persons deputed from every part of the country; and as they have thought proper to open and begin their deliberations with a solemn address unto God, and the consideration of his holy word, I most chearfully comply with their request to officiate on this occasion, and shall endeavour, as I may be enabled, to point out such directions from the holy scriptures as may make us wise in the knowledge of time, and direct us how to carry ourselves worthy of the character of good subjects and Christians: Whatever may be necessary for this purpose, I take to be comprehended in the apostolical rule, which I have laid down as the subject of this discourse, " So speak, and so do, as they that shall be " judged by the law of liberty."

There are two things which properly come before us, viz.

I. That we are to be judged by the law of liberty; and

II. The exhortation to act worthy, and under the influence, of this important truth on every occasion.

A law is a rule of behaviour, made under proper authority, and with penalties annexed, suitable to deter the transgressions. As all laws suppose man to be in a social state, so all laws ought to be made for the good of man: A law that is not made by such as have
authority

authority for fo doing, is of no force; and if authority makes laws deftructive in themfelves, no authority can prevent things from finally taking their natural courfe.

Wherever there is fociety, there muft alfo be law; it is impoffible that fociety fhould fubfift without it. The will, minds, tempers, difpofitions, views and interefts of men are fo very different, and fometimes fo oppofite, that without law, which cements and binds all, every thing would be in endlefs diforder and confufion. All laws ufually wear the complexion of thofe by whom they were made, but it cannot be denied that fome bad men, from a fenfe of neceffity, have made good laws, and that fome good men, from miftake, or other weakneffes, have enacted laws bad in themfelves, and pernicious in their confequences.

All human laws partake of human imperfection; it is not fo with the laws of GOD. He is perfect, and fo are all his works and ways. " The law of the LORD " is perfect, converting the foul. The teftimony of " the LORD is fure, making wife the fimple. The " ftatutes of the LORD are right, rejoicing the heart. " The commandment of the LORD is pure, enlighten- " ing the eyes. All his judgments are truth, and " righteoufnefs altogether." Pfalm xix.

Among men every fociety and country has its own laws and form of government, which may be very different, and cannot operate beyond their limits; but thofe laws and that form of government is undoubtedly beft which has the greateft tendency to make all thofe that live under it fecure and happy. As foon as we confider man as formed into fociety, it is evident that the * fafety of the whole muft be the grand law which muft influence and direct every other: Men did not pafs from a ftate of nature into a ftate of fociety, to render

their

* Salus populi fuprema lex.

their fituation more miferable, and their rights more
precarious That government and tyranny is the hereditary right of fome, and that flavery and oppreffion is
the original doom of others, is a doctrine that would
reflect difhonour upon GOD; it is treafon againft all
mankind, it is indeed an enormous faith that millions
were made for one; tranfubftantiation is but a harmlefs
abfurdity, compared with the notion of a divine right
to govern wrong, or of making laws which are contrary to every idea of liberty, property and juftice.

The law which the apoftle fpeaks of in our text, is
not a law of man, but of Him who is the only lawgiver,
that can fave and condemn, to whom all owe obedience,
and whofe laws none can tranfgrefs with impunity.

Though all the laws that GOD ever gave unto man
are worthy of GOD, and tend to promote the happinefs of thofe to whom they were given, yet we may
obferve a very ftriking variety in the different laws
which he gave at different times and to different people.
" He fhewed his word unto Jacob, his ftatutes and
" his judgments unto Ifrael; he has not dealt fo with
" any other nation." Pfalm cxlvii : 18. 19.

To the generality of mankind he gave no written
law, but yet left not himfelf without a witnefs among
them; the words of the law were written in their hearts,
their confcience alfo bearing witnefs, and their thoughts
the mean while excufing or elfe accufing one another:
It cannot be faid they were without law, whilft what
they were to do, and what they were to forbear, was
written in their hearts.

To Ifrael GOD came with a fiery law in his hands,
it was given with the moft awful folemnity upon mount
Sinai; and as the fum and fubftance of all their ceremonial, political and moral law centered in the ten
commandments, fo the fum and fubftance of thefe is

D   compre-

comprehended in love to GOD and love to ı. which, as our LORD himself informs us, contains all the law and all the prophets.

All manifeſtations of the will of GOD have been gradual, and it is probable the means of knowing GOD will be progreſſive through different ages, till eternity gives the good man a full fight of GOD in his immediate preſence. During the diſpenſation of the old teſtament and the ceremonial law, a ſpirit of bondage obtained unto fear, the law was a ſchoolmaſter to bring us unto CHRIST; neither did the law make any thing perfect, but the bringing in of a better hope: Grace and truth was brought to light by JESUS CHRIST, and hence the diſpenſation of the goſpel, under which we live, is called the law of LIBERTY.

Though there is a manifeſt diſtinction between law and goſpel, and ſometimes theſe t. o things are even oppoſed to one another, yet the doctrine of the goſpel is alſo called " the law of faith;" Rom. iii: 17. partly becauſe it was uſual with the Jewiſh writers to call every doctrine a law, and partly alſo becauſe the doctrine of the goſpel preſents us with a rule of life, which all its profeſſors are bound to obey; hence they are ſaid to be " not without law, but under the law of CHRIST;" 1 Cor. ix: 11. and hence our apoſtle ſpeaks of a royal law, which, though we cannot obey in perfection, nor derive any merit from our imperfect obedience, we cannot neglect without danger, nor diſobey without ſhewing our diſregard to the doctrine of the goſpel in general.

It deſerves very particular attention that the doctrine of the goſpel is called a law of LIBERTY. Liberty and law are perfectly conſiſtent; liberty does not conſiſt in living without all reſtraint; for were all men to live without reſtraint, as they pleaſe, there would ſoon be no liberty at all; the ſtrongeſt w ıı be maſter, the

weakeſt

weakeſt go to the wall; right, juſtice and property
muſt give way to power, and, inſtead of its being a
bleſſing, a more unhappy ſituation could not eaſily be
deviſed unto mankind than that every man ſhould
have it in his power to do what is right in his own
eyes: well regulated liberty of individuals is the natural offſpring of laws, which prudentially regulate the
rights of whole communities; and as laws which take
away the natural rights of men, are unjuſt and oppreſ-
five, ſo all liberty which is not regulated by law, is a
deluſive phantom, and unworthy of the glorious name.

The goſpel is called a law of liberty, becauſe it bears
a moſt friendly aſpect to the liberty of man; it is a
known rule, *Evangelium non tollit politias*, the goſpel
makes no alteration in the civil ſtate; it by no means
renders man's natural and ſocial condition worſe than
it would be without the knowledge of the goſpel.
When the Jews boaſted of their freedom, and that they
never were in bondage, our LORD does not reprove
them for it, but only obſerves, that national freedom
ſtill admits of improvement: " If the Son ſhall make
" you free, then are you free indeed." John viii: 16.
This leads me to obſerve that the goſpel is a law of
liberty in a much higher ſenſe: By whomſoever a man
is overcome, of the ſame he is brought into bondage;
but no external enemy can ſo completely tyrannize over
a conquered enemy, as ſin does over all thoſe who yield
themſelves its ſervants; vicious habits, when once
they have gained the aſcendant in the ſoul, bring man
to that unhappy paſs that he knows better things and
does worſe; ſin, like a torrent, carries him away againſt
knowledge and conviction, while conſcience fully con-
vinceth him that he travels the road of death, and muſt
expect, if he ſo continues, to take up his abode in hell;
though his decaying body clearly tells him ſin breaks

D   his

his conſtitution, as well as waſtes his ſubſtance, though
he feels the loſs of credit and wealth, ſtill ſin has too
ſtrong a hold of him to be forſaken, though he faintly
reſolves to break off, yet, till the grace of GOD brings
ſalvation, when he would do good, evil is preſent with
him; in ſhort, inſtead of being under a law of liberty,
he is under the law of ſin and death, but whenever he
feels the happy influence of the grace of the goſpel,
then this "law of liberty makes him free from the
" law of ſin and death;" Rom. viii: 2. it furniſheth
him not only with motives to reſiſt but with power
alſo to ſubdue ſin; ſin reigns no longer in his mortal
body, becauſe he is not under the law, but under grace.
By this law of liberty he is made free from ſin, and has
his fruit unto holineſs, and the end of it eternal life.
There is another reaſon why the goſpel is called a law
of liberty, which is to diſtinguiſh it from the ceremonial law under the Moſaic diſpenſation; a yoke, of
which an apoſtle ſaith, neither they nor their fathers
were able to bear; it was ſuperadded on account of
their tranſgreſſions, and ſuited to the character of a
groſs and ſtubborn nation, to whom it was originally
given; they were ſo prone to idolatry, and ſo apt to
forget their GOD, their notions were ſo groſs and car-
nal, that a number of external rites and ceremonies became neceſſary, to put them in mind of him, and to
attach them to ſome degree of his worſhip and ſervice.
This, however neceſſary, was a heavy burden; it bid
them "touch not, taſte not, handle not;" it required
of them expenſive ſacrifices, and a coſtly and painful
ſervice; it was attended with the moſt fearful threatnings, if any man brake Moſes law, he died under
two or three witneſſes; and the very ſpirit they then
received, was a ſpirit of bondage unto fear: Whereas
the goſpel diſpenſation breatheth a ſpirit of confidence,
and

and under the law of liberty we call upon God as Abba
Father. By this law of liberty the profeſſors of the
goſpel will be judged.

Every man is a rational, and therefore accountable,
creature. As a creature he muſt needs depend on his
Creator, and as a rational creature he muſt certainly
be accountable for all his actions. Nothing is more
evident than that man is not of himſelf; and if once
we admit that he holds his exiſtence, his faculties and
favours from God, that made him, it becomes a very
obvious concluſion, that his Maker muſt have had ſome
view in giving him exiſtence, and more underſtanding
than to the beaſts of the field, neither can it be a matter of indifference to him whether man acts agreeably
or contrary to his deſigns. The Creator of the natural
world, is alſo its moral ruler; and if he is now the
proprietor and ruler of intelligent beings, at ſome time
or other he muſt alſo be their judge.

If God had not made his will known unto man,
there could have been neither tranſgreſſion nor judge-
ment. If it ſhould be ſaid that God has not manifeſted
himſelf alike unto all men, and that ſome have much
ſmaller opportunities to know his will and their duty
than others, it is enough to obſerve, that no man will
be judged by a rule of which it was impoſſible he
ſhould have any knowledge. Every work and every
man will be brought into judgment, and the judgment
of God will never be otherwiſe than according to truth;
but thoſe that never had the law of liberty, will not be
judged by that law, and thoſe that have been favoured
with the revelation of the goſpel will be more inexcuſable than any others, if they neglect the day of their
viſitation. "As many as have ſinned without law, ſhall
" alſo periſh without law, and as many as have ſinned
" in the law, ſhall be judged by the law." Rom. ii: 12.

All

All men are under some law, they feel. they are conscious, that they are so; the thoughts which already excuse or condemn one another, are an anticipation of a final and decisive judgment, when every man's reward will be according to his works.

That all those who heard and professed to believe the gospel, will be finally judged by that, we have the fullest assurance. God will judge the secrets of men by JESUS CHRIST according to his gospel. " The word " that I have spoken," saith CHRIST, "the same will " judge them that heard it, on the last day." John xii: 48. It greatly interests us clearly to know what is the import and consequence of being judged by the gospel as a law of liberty; and it contains the following things,

The general character, all the thoughts, words and actions, together with the general conduct of all those who professed the gospel, will be brought to the test, and tried by this rule. Man's own opinion of himself, the good opinion of others, will here stand him in no stead; his character will not be determined by his external appearance, but by his inward reality. " Man " looketh on the outward appearance, but the LORD " looketh on the heart." 1 Sam. xvii: 7. The self-righteous pharisee will be rejected, notwithstanding his fair appearance and boasting; the penitent publican will be received, though he has nothing to plead but LORD have mercy on me a sinner. The law is spiritual, and no law more so than the law of the gospel; it requires not merely an external obedience, but an internal conformity to the will of God; it demands truth in the inward part, it looks not only to the actions that are done, but to the principle from which they flow; we must judge of man's inward disposition by his visible action, but God judges of the actions of men according

cording to their invifible fpring; thoughts are out of the
reach of human cognizance, but they are the firft object of divine notice; there is not a word that drops
from our tongue but what our judge hears, whatever
we do, or whatever we neglect, is all under his immediate eye, and he not only attends to our general character, but alfo to every thought, word or action, and
the prevailing complexion of all thefe taken together
form our true and real character.

In the judgment, according to this law, our character, words, thoughts and actions will be brought to
the teft of this rule, our conduct will be compared
with thefe precepts, this is the balance of the fanctuary,
in which the profeffors of the gofpel fhall be weighed,
and as they fhall be found approved or deficient, their
cafe muft be determined. Thofe whofe temper and
actions fhall be found conformable to the law of liberty, will be acquitted, gracioufly accepted, and made
ever happy, and thofe who turned the grace of GOD
into wantonnefs, and made the liberty of the gofpel a
cloak for their fins, will be finally rejected. The gofpel
informs us, that a day is already appointed for that
purpofe; it acquaints us with the perfon of our judge,
and every circumftance, as well as the rule according
to which he will proceed in judgment. Perhaps on
that day when all nations fhall appear before the judge,
and he will divide them as a fhepherd divideth the
fheep from the goats, diftinct places will alfo be al-
lotted to thofe who are to be judged by natural confcience and the law of nature, and thofe who have been
favoured with a divine revelation, and efpecially with
the light of the gofpel: The people of Niniveh will
arife againft empty profeffors of the gofpel, and will
condemn them. Thofe who have been exalted above
others in means and privileges, will fit proportionably
lower

lower than thofe who have made a better improvement of leffer means; and notwithftanding the fondeft hope and fineft profeffion, it is a determined rule of the law of liberty, that " except our righteoufnefs " fhall exceed that of the fcribes and pharifees, we " fhall in no cafe enter into the kingdom of heaven."

It deferves our peculiar attention, that the apoftle confiders the gofpel as a law of liberty, at the fame time when he fets it before us as the rule by which we are to be judged. We are not to imagine becaufe the gofpel is a law of liberty, therefore men will not be judged; on the contrary judgment will be the more fevere againft all who have heard and profeffed the gofpel, and yet walked contrary to its precepts and doctrine. As the tranfgreffion of a law of liberty muft be more inexcufable, than the tranfgreffion of a law unjuft or oppreffive in itfelf, or even the ceremonial law, which was given only for a certain period, and to anfwer temporary purpofes, fo their judgment and doom muft be proportionably heavier, who have finned againft love and liberty, as well as againft power and juftice.

According to this law the fate of men will not only be determined, but fentence will alfo be put into execution. God fitteth on the throne of judgment every day, and judgeth righteoufly, but he hath moreover appointed a particular day when he will manifeft his power and juftice before the whole creation; when the dead both fmall and great will ftand before God; when thofe that acted agreeable to the law of liberty, will attain the fulnefs of glory of the freedom of the fons of God, and when he will alfo take vengeance on all that have not known God, and have not obeyed his holy gofpel. This naturally leads to the fecond thing propofed, to take a nearer view of the importance of

the

the exhortation, " So fpeak, and fo do, as they that " fhall be judged by the law of liberty."

It feems as though the apoftle had an eye to fome particular branch of the law of liberty, *i. e.* the love which we owe unto our neighbour, and that his defign is to obviate the miftake as though men might be con- fidered as fulfilling the law of CHRIST, in paying re- fpect to fome of its commands and prohibitions, at the fame time that they were entirely regardlefs of the reft. He affures them, that " whofoever fhall keep the " whole law, but fhall tranfgrefs in one point " (*e. g.* having refpect of perfons) " is guilty of all." On this principle the apoftle builds the general exhortation, " So fpeak, and fo do, as they that fhall be judged " by the law of liberty." This implies :

1. Be thoroughly convinced of the certainty of a judg- ment to come, and that it extends to you, to all your thoughts, words and actions. There is not any truth of greater moment, nor perhaps more eafily forgotten. The belief or unbelief of this important doctrine muft have the moft fenfible effects. All the apoftles fre- quently put their hearers in mind of a judgment to come ; and there is not any truth more neceffary to be frequently inculcated and daily thought on, and wherever this truth is really believed and felt, it will have a conftant and natural influence on the behaviour of thofe who truly believe it.

2. See to it that in judgment you may ftand. All men will be brought into judgment, but few will be able to ftand ; none will be excufed, or be able to withdraw, and only thofe who have acted worthily, will meet with the divine acceptance. The difference will be amazing and beyond all conception : An eternity of happinefs, which eye has not feen, ear has not heard, and which never entered into the heart of any man, lies on the

E one

one fide, and defpair, mifery and torment on the other. Thofe that are able to ftand, will meet with the fmiles and approbation of their judge, and to all the reft the king will fay, " Thefe mine enemies that " would not have me to bear rule over them, bring " them here, and flay them before mine eyes." Thofe that believe and are convinced of this awful alternative, fhould certainly make it their care that they may be able to ftand in judgment; neither fhould the per-fuafion of this only influence their conduct in general, but thefe words ought to be confidered as a rule, which we ought to have conftantly before our eyes in all our difcourfes and every undertaking; we fhould ever " fo " fpeak, and fo act, as they that fhall be judged by " the law of liberty."

I fhall draw a few inferences, before I conclude with a more particular addrefs to the worthy Gentlemen at whofe requeft I preach on this occafion.

1. *The gofpel is a law of Liberty.*

A late writer * afferts, " Every religion counte-" nances defpotifm, but none fo much as the Chriftian." This is a very heavy charge againft religion in gene-ral, but bears hardeft on the Chriftian. Whether it proceeds from malice, ignorance, or mifapprehenfion, it is needlefs to determine; but if chriftianity be a law of liberty, it muft be obvious how ill-grounded is fuch a charge againft it. It cannot be denied but fome Chriftian writers have wrote againft the rights of man-kind. All thofe who ftand up for unlimited paffive obedience and non-refiftance, may have given but too much caufe for fuch furmifes and fufpicions; but the truth is, that both thofe which make this charge, and thofe who gave occafion for it, were alike ignorant of the fpirit and temper of Chriftianity; and it may well be

* See a tract, entituled, " Chains of flavery." Printed London. 1775.

be doubted whether the venders of such odious doctrines, who foisted tenets, so abominable and injurious to mankind, into the system of Christian religion, have not done that holy religion greater hurt under the pretence of friendship and defence than its most barefaced enemies by all their most violent attacks. Some Christian divines have taught the enormous faith, that millions were made for one, they have ascribed a divine right to kings to govern wrong; but what then? Are such abominable doctrines any part of christianity, because these men say so? does the gospel cease to be a law of liberty, because some of its professors pervert it into an engine of tyranny, oppression and injustice.

The assertion, that all religion countenances despotism, and christianity more than any other, is diametrically opposite to fact. Survey the globe, and you will find that liberty has taken its seat only in Christendom, and that the highest degree of freedom is pleaded for and enjoyed by such as make profession of the gospel.

There are but two religions, which are concerned in this charge; the Jewish and the Christian. Natural religion writers of this kind I suppose would not include in their charge; if they do, they set all religion at variance with the rights of mankind, contrary to the sense of all nations, who are generally agreed, that, abstractly of a world to come, religion is of real service and necessity to mankind, for their better government and order.

As to the Jewish religion, it seems really strange that any should charge it with favouring despotism, when by one of its express rites at certain times it proclaimed " liberty throughout the land, to the inha-
" bitants thereof." Levit. xxv : 10. It required their

kings

kings " not to be lifted up in their hearts above their
" brethren." Deut. xvii : 20 And the whole fyftem of
that religion is fo replete with laws againft injuftice
and oppreffion, it pays fuch an extraordinary regard
to property, and gives fuch ftrict a charge to rule in
juftice and the fear of GOD, and to confider thofe,
over whom they judge, as their brethren, even when
difpenfing punifhments, and forbids all excefs in them,
that it is really furprizing any one acquainted with its
precepts, fhould declare it favourable to defpotifm or
oppreffion.

The Chriftian religion, while it commands due refpect and obedience to fuperiors, no where requires a
blind and unlimited obedience on the part of the fubjects ; nor does it veft any abfolute and arbitrary power
in the rulers. It is an inftitution for the benefit, and
not for the diftrefs, of mankind. It preacheth not only
" glory to GOD on high," but alfo " peace on earth,
" and good will among men."

The gofpel gives no higher authority to magiftrates
than to be " the minifters of GOD, for the good of
" the fubject." Rom. xiii. From whence it muft furely
follow, that their power is to edify, and not to deftroy :
When they abufe their authority, to diftrefs and deftroy their fubjects, they deferve not to be thought
minifters of GOD for good ; nor is it to be fuppofed,
when they act fo contrary to the nature of their office,
that they act agreeable to the will of GOD, or in conformity to the doctrine of the gofpel.

The gofpel recommends unto mafters to forbear
threatnings, and to remember that they alfo have a
mafter in heaven ; it affures them that the eye of GOD
is equally upon the fervant and the mafter, and that
with GOD there is no refpect of perfons : It commands
mafters, from the moft folemn confiderations, to give
unto

unto fervants that which is juft and equal; it faith to
the meaneft flave: "Art thou called being a fervant,
"care not for it, but if thou mayeft be made free, ufe
"it rather." 1 Cor. vii: 21.

The doctrine of the gofpel has that regard to property, that it commands even foldiers, "Do violence
"to no man, and be content with your wages:" Luke
iii: 14.—that a Paul fent back a run-away flave, though
now converted, and belonging to his intimate friend,
and at a time when he feems to have ftood in real need
of his fervice, from a delicacy that he would do nothing
without the owner's mind, lefs his benefit fhould appear as if it were of neceffity, and not willingly. Phi-
lem. 14. From the fame fpirit of juftice a Zacheus,
after his converfion, reftored fourfold what before he
had taken from any by falfe accufation: Surely then
the fpirit of the gofpel is very friendly to the rights
and property of men.

The gofpel fets confcience above all human authority in matters of faith, and bids us to "ftand faft
"in that liberty wherewith the Son of God has made
"us free." Gal. v: 1. Freedom is the very fpirit and
temper of the gofpel: "He that is called in the
"Lord being a fervant, is the Lord's freeman.
"Ye are bought with a price, be ye not the fervants
"of men." 1 Cor. vii: 22. 23. At the fame time that
it commands us to fubmit to every ordinance of men,
it alfo directs us to act "as free, and not ufing liberty
"as a cloke of malicioufnefs, but as the fervants of
"God." 1 Pet. iii: 13-18.

Thofe therefore that would fupport arbitrary power,
and require an unlimited obedience, in vain look for
precedents or precepts for fuch things in the gofpel,
an inftitution equally tending to make men juft, free

and

and happy here, and perfectly holy and happy hereafter.

2. *The main design of the gospel is not to direct us in
our external and civil affairs, but how we may at last
stand with comfort before* GOD, *the judge of all.*

Human prudence is to be our guide in the concerns
of time; the gospel makes us wise unto salvation, and
points out the means to be pursued that it may be
well with us in the world to come. As rational creatures
we are to make use of our reason; as Christians we
are to repent and believe the gospel. Motives of a
worldly nature may very properly influence us in our
worldly concern, we are created not only for eternity,
but also for time: It is not at all improper for us to
have a due regard for both. The gospel will regulate
our desires and restrain our passions as to earthly
things, and will raise us at the same time above time
and sense, to objects of a nature more worthy of ourselves. A due regard for, and frequent meditation on,
a judgment to come, will greatly assist us in all our
concerns; and this very consideration the gospel holds
out to us in the clearest manner. It not only affirms
as a truth, what reason and conscience might consider
only as probable, but it takes away as it were the veil
from between us and things to come; it gives us a
present view of the future bliss of saints, and the
terrors and despair of sinners; —— rather a historical account than a prophetic description of all the
proceedings of the dreadful pleasing day; it clearly
points out the road to destruction, and the way to
escape; it affords us a plain and general rule to obtain
safety and comfort, when it bids us, " So speak, and
" so do, as they that shall be judged by the law of
" liberty."

This general rule may also be of considerable service
in

in extraordinary and particular cafes. It is impoffible to provide exprefs directions for every particular cafe, and in the courfe of things circumftances may happen when a good man may be at a lofs to know his duty, and find it difficult fo to act as to obtain his own approbation. There may be danger of going beyond, and danger in not coming up to, the mark. To act worthy of GOD, who has called us, is the general rule of the Chriftian at all times, and upon every occafion, and did we but always follow this rule, what manner of perfons fhould we then be ! But in cafes of intricacy we may ftill be in doubt what may be moft for the glory of GOD, and moft confiftent with our duty. Sometimes alfo our relative duties may feem to come in competition with one another, and we may hefitate in our own mind which for the prefent has the ftrongeft call. We would fain obey our fuperiors, and yet we cannot think of giving up our natural, our civil and religious rights, nor acquiefce in or contribute to render our fellow-creatures or fellow-citizens flaves and miferable. We would willingly follow peace with all men, and yet would be very unwilling that others fhould take the advantage of a pacific difpofition, to injure us in hopes of impunity. We would exprefs duty, refpect and obedience to the king, as fupreme, and yet we would not wifh to ftrengthen the hands of tyranny, nor call oppreffion lawful : In fuch a delicate fituation it is a golden rule, " So to fpeak, and fo to do, as they " that fhall be judged by the law of liberty." Nothing has a greater tendency to make men act wrong than the difbelief of a future judgment, and nothing will more effectually reftrain and direct them than the full perfuafion that fuch an event will certainly take place; nothing would have a happier tendency to make us act with prudence, juftice and moderation than the

firm

firm perfuafion that GoD will bring every work into judgment, and every fecret thing, whether it be good or bad.

Neither could I think on any direction more applicable to the defign of our prefent meeting, or which I might more properly recommend to the refpectable Gentlemen, now met together to confult on the recovery and prefervation of the liberties of America, and who chofe to begin their deliberations with a folemn act of worfhip to almighty GoD who has eftablifhed government as his ordinance, and equally abhors licentioufnefs and oppreffion; whofe fingular bleffing it is if fubjects enjoy a righteous governmeӿt, and under fuch a government lead a quiet and peaceable life in all godlinefs and honefty.

You are met, Gentlemen, in a moft critical time, and on a moft alarming occafion, not in a legiflative capacity, but (while the fitting of the ufual reprefentation is not thought for the king's fervice, or neceffary for the good of this province) you are chofen by the general voice of this province to meet on their behalf, to confult on fuch meafures as in our local circumftances may be moft to the real advantage and tend to the honour of our gracious fovereign, as well as the good and fafety of this province and of all this great continent. For the fake of the auditory, I fhall briefly ftate the immediate caufes that have given rife to this Provincial and a general American Congrefs, and then offer fuch humble advice as appears to me moft fuitable to our circumftances.

To enforce fome Acts for laying on a duty to raife a perpetual revenue in America, which the Americans think unjuft and unconftitutional, which all America complains of, and fome provinces have in fome meafure oppofed.

oppofed.* A fleet and army has been fent to New-England, and after a long feries of hardfhips by that province patiently endured, it is now out of all quc-ftion that hoftilities have been commenced againft them; blood has been fhed, and many lives have been taken away; thoufands, never as much as fufpected of having any hand in the action which is made the pretence of all the feverity now ufed againft that province, have been and ftill are reduced to the greateft diftrefs. From this other provinces have taken the alarm; an apprehenfion of nearer foes, not unlikely to appear as auxiliaries in an unjuft caufe, has thrown our neighbours into arms; how far and wide the flame fo wantonly kindled may be permitted to fpread, none can tell; but in thefe alarming circumftances the liberty of this continent, of which we are a part, the fafety and domeftic peace of this province will naturally become a fubject of your deliberations; and here I may well adapt the language of old, " There was no " fuch deed done nor feen from the day that America " was firft fettled unto this day; confider of it, take " advice, and fpeak your minds." Judges xix: 30. I m an not to anticipate and direct your counfels, but from your defire I fhould fpeak on this occafion; I take it for granted you will permit me to offer fuch hints as may appear fuitable to the place and defign of our prefent meeting.

In the firft place, as there is no evil in a city in which tne hand of GoD may not be feen, fo in vain is

F   falvation

---

* This oppofition in fome provinces confifted in fending the tea on which this duty was to be paid, back to England, not fuffering it to be fold or landed in others, and in Bofton, when they were prevented from fending it back, it was entirely deftroyed, but no perfon hurt, nor any blood fhed.

salvation looked for from the hills and from the mountains, but can come from him only who has made heaven and earth. This undoubtedly is a day of trouble, but GOD faith to his people, " Call upon me " in a day of trouble, and I will deliver thee." Pf. l: 15. " What nation has GOD fo nigh unto them, as the " LORD our GOD is in all things that we call upon " him for." Deut. iv: 7. If this be our firft ftep, if firft of all we look unto him from whom our help cometh, we may hope all will be well at laft. Let us be thoroughly convinced of this, we muft ftand well with GOD, elfe it can never be well with us at all ; without him and his help we can never profper. The LORD is with you, if you are with him.; " if you feek him, " you will find him, but if you forfake him, you will " be forfaken by him." 2 Chron. xv: 2. If GOD be for us, who can be againft us ? if he be againft us, who can be for us ? Before we think on, or look any where elfe, may our eyes be unto GOD, that he may be gracious unto us. Let us humbly confefs and fpeedily turn from our fins, deprecate his judgment, and fecure his favour. " Rent your hearts, and not " your garments, and turn unto the LORD your GOD, " for he is gracious and merciful, flow to anger and " of great kindnefs, and repenteth him of the evil, " who knoweth if he will return and repent, and leave " a blefling behind him, even a meat-offering and a " drink-offering unto the LORD your GOD." Joel ii: 13. 14.

Let it be a ftanding rule with every one that is to fit in council upon this occafion, " fo to fpeak, and fo " to do, as one that is to be judged by the law of li- " berty " Let us moft carefully avoid every thing that might make us incur the difpleafure of GOD, and

wound

wound our own confciences. The effects of your deli-
beration may become very ferious and extenfive, and
the confequences extremely important : Think therefore before you fpeak, deliberate before you execute,
and let the law of liberty, by which you are hereafter
to be judged, be the conftant rule of all your words
and actions : Far be it from us to be reduced under
laws inconfiftent with liberty, and as far to wifh for
liberty without law; let the one be fo tempered with
the other that when we come to give our account to
the fupreme lawgiver, who is the great judge of all,
it may appear we had a due regard to both, and may
meet with his approbation.

Such always hath been, and fuch is ftill, the attachment of America to the illuftrious houfe of Hanover,
that I need not put you in mind of our duty to the
king as fupreme. By our law the king can do no wrong;
but of his prefent Majefty, who is univerfally known
to be adorned with many focial virtues, may we not
juftly conclude that he would not do any wrong, even
though he could. May we not hope that to the greatnefs of a monarch, he will fuperadd the feelings of the
man, the tendernefs of a father. May we not hope
that when the truth of things, the tears of his fuffering fubjects, the diftreffes caufed by Acts extremely
ill advifed, once reach his notice, a generous pity will
force his heart, and that pity, when he feels it, will
command redrefs. " The heart of the king is in the hand
" of the LORD, as the rivers of water, and he turneth
" it as he pleafeth ;" Prov. xxi: 1. moft earneftly therefore let us pray that in this great and moft important
matter alfo GOD may give unto the king an underftanding heart, that power may be governed by wif-

dom,

dom, and the wheels of government roll on with juſtice
and moderation.

Should you think that all our preſent diſtreſs is
owing to evil counſellors, nothing need to hinder you
from praying that GOD would turn their counſels into
fooliſhneſs; you may make it your earneſt requeſt both
in public and in private, that the wicked being removed
from before the king, his throne may be eſtabliſhed
in righteouſneſs, that the rod of the oppreſſor may be
broke, and juſtice and equity take place of tyranny
and oppreſſion.

It may be owing to nothing but the firm attachment
to the reigning family that ſo many Americans look
upon the preſent meaſures as a deep laid plan to bring
in the Pretender. Perhaps this jealouſy may be very
groundleſs, but ſo much is certain, that none but
Great Britain's enemies can be gainers in this unnatural conteſt.*

Never let us looſe out of ſight that our intereſt lies
in a perpetual connection with our mother country.
Notwithſtanding the preſent unwiſe and harſh meaſures,
there are thouſands in Great-Britain that think with
us, and wiſh well to the American cauſe, and make it
their own; let us convince our enemies that the ſtrug-
gles of America have not their riſe in a deſire of independency, but from a warm regard to our common
conſtitution; that we eſteem the name of Britons, as
being the ſame with freemen; let every ſtep we take
afford proof how greatly we eſteem our mother country,
and

* Were it deſigned to give the Pretender an opportunity; to raiſe
diviſions in Great-Britain, ſtarve the manufacturers, ſend away
troops from Ireland and Scotland, and breed civil war in America,
muſt all be circumſtances too favourable, and I may ſay, very tempt-
ing to promote ſuch a project.

and that, to the wifh of a perpetual connexion, we pre-
fer this only confideration, that we may be virtuous
and free †

Let me intreat you, Gentlemen, think coolly, and
act deliberately; rafh counfels are feldom good ones:
minifterial rafhnefs and American rafhnefs can only be
productive of untoward compounds; inconfiderate
meafures, framed on the other fide of the atlantic, are
the caufe of all our mifchiefs, and it is not in the leaft
probable that inconfiderate meafures in America can
be productive of any good. Let nothing be done
through ftrive and vain glory; let no private refentment or party zeal difgrace your honeft warmth for
your country's welfare: Meafures determined on by
integrity and prudence, are moft likely to be carried
into execution by fteadinefs and moderation. Let
neither the frowns of tyranny, nor pleafure of popularity, fway you from what you clearly apprehend juft
and right, and to be your duty. Confider how much
lies at ftake, how greatly your religion, your liberty,
your property, your pofterity, is interefted. Endeavour
to act like freemen, like loyal fubjects, like real Chri-
ftians,

† The idea of a feparation between America and Great-Britain
is big with fo many and fuch horrid evils, that every friend to both
muft fhudder at the thought. Every man that gives the moft diftant
hint of fuch a wifh, ought inftantly to be fufpected as a common
enemy; nothing would more effectually ferve the caufe of our enemies, than any propofal of this kind; all wife men and all good
men would immediately fpeak, write and act againft it; fuch a propofal, whenever it fhould be made, would be an inlet to greater
evils than any we have yet fuffered: But what America detefts as
the greateft evil, a Britifh miniftry has taken the greateft pains to
effect; has wafted Britifh blood and treafure to alienate America
and Great Britain; the breach is growing wider and wider, it is be
come great like a fea, every moment is a lofs that is not improved
towards bringing about a reconciliation.

ftians, and you will " fo fpeak, and fo act, as they that " fhall be judged by the law of liberty." - Act con-fcientioufly, and with a view to God, then commit your ways to him, leave the event with God, and you will have great reafon to hope that the event will be juft, honourable and happy.

And now, Gentlemen, you have the wifhes and prayers of every thoughtful perfon, that your delibera-tions may be carried on with candour, unanimity and prudence, may be bleffed to preferve the quietnefs of this province, and co-operate in reftoring the rights and tranquillity of all America, as well as promote the profperity of the whole Britifh empire. This will af-ford you a heartfelt fatisfaction, and tranfmit your name to pofterity with honour, when all thofe who had oppofite views, and fought their greatnefs in the ruins of others, will be held in abhorrence and deteftation.

I have but a few hints to give to my hearers in general.

The times are evil; this is a day of adverfity, and in a time of adverfity we ought to confider. It may perhaps foon become impoffible, even to the moft in-dolent, to continue unconcerned, and thofe that wifh no more than to hide themfelves in quiet obfcurity, may not always have it in their power to remain neuter: To know the figns of the time, is a confiderable part of human prudence, and it is a ftill greater to walk circumfpectly, and redeem the time, becaufe the days are evil. Whatever part you may think yourfelves obliged to take, " So fpeak, and fo do, as they that " fhall be judged hereafter, and judged by the law of " liberty."

In thefe times of confufion I would prefs on my
                                                    hearers

hearers a moſt conſcientious regard to the common laws of the land. Let our conduct ſhew that we are not lawleſs; by well-doing let us put to ſilence the reproaches of our adverſaries. Let us convince them that we do not complain of law, but of oppreſſion; that we do not abhor theſe acts becauſe we are impatient to be under government, but being deſtructive of liberty and property, we think them deſtructive alſo of all law. Let us act " as free, and yet not " make liberty a cloke of malicioufneſs, but as the " ſervants of God."

While it is yet peace and quietneſs with us, let us not think ourſelves inacceſſible to the evils which are already come upon others; there are ſome evils which we would rather deprecate in private than ſpeak of in public, againſt which being forewarned, we ſhould be forearmed; every trifling report ſhould not alarm us, but it would be folly ſtill greater not to be on our guard againſt ſudden dangers.

Remember them that ſuffer adverſity, as being yourſelves alſo in the body. Think on thoſe who are driven from their habitations and all their conveniencies of life, or confined in their own houſes by an enraged ſoldiery, to ſtarve in their own country, in the midſt of property and plenty, not permitted to enjoy their own, and diſtreſſed in every connexion, and this without any cauſe alleged againſt numbers of them, without complaint, ſuſpicion or a legal trial: The like was never heard ſince the cruel ſiege of Londonderry, and is a ſpecies of cruelty at which even that hardhearted bigot James II. relented.

Above all, let every one earneſtly pray that HE that is higher than the higheſt would ſoon make a righteous end of all their confuſion; that he would

incline

incline the king to hear the cries of his fubjects, and that no more innocent blood may be fhed in America.

One thing more: Confider the extreme abfurdity of ftruggling for civil liberty, and yet to continue flaves to fin and luft. "Know ye not to whom ye "yield yourfelves fervants to obey, his fervants ye "are, to whom ye obey, whether of fin unto death, "or of obedience unto righteoufnefs." Rom. vi: 16. Ceafe from evil, and do good, feek peace, and purfue it, who will hurt you while you follow that which is good; become the willing fervants of the LORD JESUS CHRIST, hearken to and obey the voice of his gofpel; for "where the fpirit of the LORD is, there "is liberty;" and "if the Son makes you free, THEN, and not till then, "SHALL YOU BE FREE INDEED."

From the fimilarity of the fubject, an extract from another fermon is added:

THE queftion between Great-Britain and America, which has already been productive of fuch alarming effects, is, "Whether the parliament of "Great-Britain have any power or authority to tax "the Americans without their confent?" Every impartial man will allow that this is the foundation of the whole difpute. It is evident that in this queftion confcience is deeply interefted, and in this view it becomes a very proper fubject for the pulpit. If any thing is required of fubjects which in confcience they are bound to pay, give or do, the refufal of it is not only a crime againft the ftate, but alfo a fin againft GOD: I think it therefore not only not improper, but

my

my duty, to point out unto my hearers fuch hints and precedents as may illuftrate this matter from the word of God.

The cafe I would ftate thus, "Whether any duty "or impoft fuppofed to be laid on in an illegal man- "ner, and inconfiftent with natural and civil rights, "from motives of confcience ought neverthelefs to be "paid?" and to elucidate this, I obferve, the general rule is this: "Render therefore to all their dues; tri- "bute to whom tribute is due, cuftom to whom cu- "ftom; fear to whom fear, honour to whom honour." Rom. xiii: 7. There is fomething *due* to government which cannot be refufed without injuftice, and more than which cannot be demanded without tyranny and oppreffion. When our Lord was afked, "What "thinkeft thou, is it lawful to give tribute unto Cefar "or not?" he gave a very wife and general anfwer, "Render therefore unto Cefar the things which are "Cefar's, and unto God the things which are God's." Matth. xxii: 17. 21. We are informed, that upon another occafion he paid the tribute-money, and that, after afking Peter of whom do the kings of the earth take cuftom or tribute? and Peter anfwering of ftrangers, he remarked, "Then are the children free;" and yet neverthelefs, as a voluntary act, ordered Peter, "Take a piece of money, and give unto them, for "me and thee." Matth. xvii: 25-27.

On thefe paffages I fhall make but two remarks, which are very obvious, and will apply themfelves: 1. How far foever the power of the magiftrate and the fubmiffion of the fubject may be extended, it is plain that by thefe rules and precedents property is left to the fub- ject. To render, give, or pay, fuppofes property. Thofe who may be juftly deprived of what they poffefs, at

another's

another's pleafure, cannot be faid to be poffeffed of any
property; and therefore they can neither give, pay, or
render; they are themfelves the property of another. I
would further obferve, 2. That from the anfwer our
Lord gives unto Peter, it appears that fovereigns ought
to treat their fubjects as children, and that children
ought to be free. O the free and benevolent fpirit of
the gofpel!

By fome it is urged, that fovereigns have a right
to take away what their fubjects poffefs, at pleafure.
This right they ground on the following paffage, 1 Sam.
viii: 10—" This will be the manner of the king that
" fhall reign over you, he will take your fons, and ap-
" point them for himfelf, for his chariots, and to be
" horfemen, and fome fhall run before his chariots—
" and he will take your daughters, to be confectionaries
" and to be cooks and bakers; and he will take your
" fields, and your vineyards, and your oliveyards, even
" the beft of them, and give them to his fervants; and
" he will take the tenth of your feed, and of your vine-
" yards, and give to his officers and his fervants; and
" he will take your men-fervants and your maid-fer-
" vants, and your goodlieft young men, and your affes,
" and put them to his work; he will take the tenth of
" your fheep, and *ye fhall be his fervants.*" Here then,
according to fome, is the warrant of divine right for
arbitrary power. Thofe however, who found authority
to do what is wrong in a reprefentation, meant to deter
the Jews from putting it in any man's power to treat
them thus, would do well to confider that from the
text itfelf it plainly appears, this was not to be confidered as a right, but as a grievance, which their folly
had brought on themfelves. " You fhall cry in that
" day, and the Lord will not hear you." Your mifery
will

will be the effect of your own folly. We have another precedent, which feems fomewhat in point: Rehoboam was a foolifh fon of a wife father ; it feems he
laid a tribute on Ifrael: (2 Chron. xiii: 18.) The
people applied unto him, prefented their grievances, and
prayed redrefs: "Thy father made our yoke grievous,
"now therefore do thou make it lighter, and we will
"ferve thee." This the council of the old men advifed him to do; they faid, "If thou wilt fpeak good
"words unto them, they will be thy fervants forever."
But more violent counfels prevailed, the acts were en-
forced, "I will add to your yoke, I will chaftife you
"with fcorpions." This the deluded monarch probably
confidered as firmnefs and dignity ; but what was
the event? When all Ifrael faw that the king hearkened
not unto them, they faid, "What portion have we in
"David? to your tents, o Ifrael! now fee to thine
"own houfe David." A kind and juft anfwer might
have prevented this ; and what did the king himfelf
gain? "The king fent Adoram, who was over the tribute, and all Ifrael ftoned him, that he died, and the
king fled to Jerufalem" Thus far tyranny was very
unfuccefsful. But this is not all; when the army of
Judah was now ready to fall upon the ten tribes, GOD
himfelf interpofed, "Ye fhall not fight againft your
"brethren, the children of Ifrael; return every man
"to his houfe, for this thing is of me." Thus this
matter ended in a feparation of the two kingdoms, and
this very Roboam himfelf afterwards became a fervant,
and tributary to the king of Egypt.

I leave the application of all thefe things to thofe
whom it may concern; but would further obferve,

Every government muft be fupported, and what is
neceffary for the fupport of government, is alfo juftly
G 2   due,

due, and ought to be GIVEN with readinefs and willingly.

Thofe that think their fuperiors have a right to take away their property, or any part of it, without their confent, upon their own principle are guilty of finful refiftance and rebellion, if they do not comply with whatever government may demand.* Thofe that think, every government has no further right than according to the laws and conftitution of its refpective country, fhould be very careful neverthelefs to obey not only for wrath, but alfo for confcience fake, and under whatever grievances they may labour never to make ufe of any methods of redrefs unjuft in themfelves, nor of any remedies that may be worfe than the difeafe.

A SHORT

* King James the Firft afked the bifhops Nelfon and Andrews, whether he had a right to raife money on his own authority ? The former affirmed it, becaufe your Majefty is the anointed of the LORD, and the breath of our noftrils. The latter replied, " I think " your Majefty has a good right to my brother Nelfon's money."

A SHORT AND CONCISE ACCOUNT OF THE STRUGGLES OF *SWISSER-LAND* FOR LIBERTY.

TO a benevolent mind taking a furvev of the globe, it muſt be a very melancholy confidera:ion that liberty, which is the birthright of man, is ſtill confined to a few ſmall ſpots of our earth : All Aſia and Afric₄ are out of the queſtion ; in the ſouthern hemiſphere of America it is un-known, and aſtoniſhing pains are now taken to drive it out of this northern Continent   In Eurrpe Great-Britain is com-monly viewed as the feat of it ; but if the conjecture of the biſhop of St. Afaph be not void of foundation, even there it hath a ſickly countenance ; SWISSERLAND, by that great man, is the only country which deferves to be called free, and even Voltaire pronounceth it happy. By what means the Swifs re-covered and preferved their freedom, is the ſubject of the fol-lowing narrative.

The three countries (uſually called cantons) of Ury, Switz and Underwalden, which firſt entered into a confederacy that laid the foundation of the republic of Swiſſerland, are but of ſmall extent, all the three cantons together do not exceed ſeventy miles in length and about thirty in breadth ; they are alſo very thinly inhabited, owing to their fituation among the Alps, many of which are covered with everlaſting ſnow, and inacceſſible to man or beaſt ; it is uſually faid of the climate, that there is nine months winter and three months cold. At the time of their revolution the country was not nearly fo well cultivated as it is at preſent, and at preſent all the inhabitants of the three cantons, capable of bearing arms, are not eſtimated above 12,000 men ; a ſmall number to make head with, as they did againſt the very powerful houſe of Auſtria. Power and number do not prove the juſtice of any cauſe, and it is more honourable to be defeated in the cauſe of virtue and juſtice, than to erect trophies to injuſtice and oppreſſion. All Swiſſerland was fubjugated by Julius Cæfar ; it became after-wards fubject to different Lords, and had a nobility which
treated

treated their inferiors with great petulancy and violence. The three cantons chose Rudolph of Habsburg to be their captain, and on his being chosen Roman emperor in 1273, the nobility complained against these countries before him, and called them rebellious; but when the emperor saw their charters, he acquitted them, confirmed their privileges, and gave them governors that were not inhabitants of these countries, and were not to tyrannize over, but only from time to time to come among them, to administer justice. Thus the country was quiet, submitted to their governors; and had they been always treated with equal justice, probably would have continued so to this day, but *Nullum violentum diuturnum,* "Nothing that is violent lasts long."

After the decease of Rudolph of Habsburg, Adolphus of Nassau was chosen emperor; he confirmed their liberty, and they continued in submission to his government. Adolphus was slain in battle by the own hands of his rival, Albertus of Austria, son of Rudolph; and it has been observed that neither this Albertus, nor any that were active against Adolphus, died of a natural death.

Albertus of Austria, having a numerous family of children, projected the establishment of a new principality in Swisserland which then was a part of the empire; many imperial fiefs he apropriated to the house of Austria, purchased some jurisdictions which belonged to monasteries, and having made himself master of some strong places, he thought to subdue these three cantons also, and sent ambassadors to Ury, Switz and Underwalden, requesting that they would surrender themselves to him and the house of Austria, under many very fair promises. When his ambassadors arrived among them, the cantons produced their charters, and also sent an embassy to the emperor, praying that they might be confirmed, and that they might not be torn from the empire, and put in subjection to the then new house of Austria. Instead of being gratified, as they had hoped, they were not only refused, but the emperor also would not take the least notice of their complaints against their governors, but appointed two new governors over them, which from day to day proceeded to new and unheard of acts of violence. The design was, by such means to excite an insurrection among the inhabitants, and then, under pretence of being rebellious, to make war upon them, and entirely to
bring

bring them under the yoke. Thefe are the exprefs words of
an hiftorian, and in different times and places, tyranny makes
ufe of the fame arts. The tyranny and cruelty of thefe governors continually encreafed. At that time there lived in Underwalden an aged and honeft inhabitant, whofe name was
Henry de Melchdall. The governor ordered two oxen to be
taken from his plough, without even charging him with any
crime; the honeft man wanted at leaft to know what had
been his fault; but the governor's officer anfwered it was the
will of the governor that henceforth the peafants fhould work
in the plough themfelves, and took away the oxen by force;
the fon of the farmer, enraged at fo much injuftice and violence, gave the officer a blow with a ftick, and wounded his
finger, and then fled the country immediately. The governor
put his aged father in prifon, and wanted to oblige him to deliver up his fon; he excufed himfelf that he did not know
what became of him, but the governor ordered both his eyes
to be put out, and took from him all he had.

The caftle of Rozberg was occupied by the governor's de-
puty of the family of Wolfenfhiefs, the fame feeing a very
handfome woman, wanted to conftrain her to gratify his bru-
tal luft; under fome pretence fhe withdrew, met her hufband,
who being informed of it, gave the governor a back-ftroke
with an axe, and alfo immediately fled the country.

Werner Stauffacre, a refpectable man in the canton Switz,
was building a handfome new houfe; the governor riding by,
enquired of him whofe it was? Stauffacre, aware of fome defign if he fhould dare to call it his own, replied, My noble
governor, the houfe belongs to my king and you, and it is
my fief. This fruftrated the governor's defign, but he told
him withall, I will not fuffer it that peafants fhould build
houfes for themfelves as though they were lords, I will bridle
you more clofely.

Governor Grisler, of Ury, could not help perceiving the
diffatisfaction of the people, and that he might difcover the
malecontents, he placed a hat on a pole at Altdorff, and
gave ftrict orders, that every one fhould pay that hat the fame
honour as if he were prefent himfelf; he alfo placed fome
fpies to obferve who fhould pay obeifance to his hat and who
fhould neglect it. This infolence wrought fo effectually on
the people, that even fome of the nobility declared it impoffible

fible any longer to endure fuch tyrannical proceedings. Among numbers that thought fo in their hearts, there was one that had courage to refufe fubmiffion to fuch a badge of abject flavery. William Tell paffed feveral times without pulling his hat; he was informed againft, and after fome imprifonment, condemned, at the diftance of one hundred and twenty yards, with his bow and arrow to take off an apple off the head of a beloved child of his, about fix years old, and threatened with death in cafe he miffed. No remonftrance availed, his life and that of his fon was threatened in cafe of refufal; the afflicted parent moft tenderly took his leave of his child, the fpectators melted in tears, but he providentially hit the apple without doing any injury to his child. This happened October 30, 1307; and romantic as it may feem, public monuments to this day confirm the truth of the fact. The people congratulated Tell on his fuccefs; but the governor obferving he had another arrow in his quiver, afked him the meaning. Tell at firft excufed himfelf with the common cuftom of marksmen: but this not fatisfying the governor, and he folemnly promifing him his life if he fhould declare the truth, Tell very frankly faid, that had he had the misfortune to have done any injury to his child, he was determined to fend the next arrow to the heart of the tyrannical governor. The governor condemned him to imprifonment for the reft of his days. Tell was permitted to bid farewell to his family, and then bound to be carried acrofs a lake to the place of his captivity, and in the fame veffel the governor alfo paffed with his attendants. The lake of Lucerne is very liable to fevere and fudden tempefts. a ftorm of this kind brought them all into the moft immediate danger: in this extremity Tell, who was known to be a good pilot, was ordered to take the helm, and he laboured fo effectually that he brought the veffel near the fhore; which he had no fooner effected, than he jumped out, and pufhed the veffel off. The governor, with great difficulty, landed at fome diftance, but in the way to his caftle he was waylaid by Tell in a narrow road, who placed the referved arrow in his heart that he inftantly fell dead from the horfe; and Tell had time to fly to fome of his friends. and give them notice of this event. Thefe were Werner Stauffacre, Walter Fürft and Arnold de Melchdall; thefe were partly forry to hear of this event, as it had been agreed upon to do nothing

before

before the firft of January, 1308, when an attempt to recover
liberty was to be made by the three cantons at once; they
apprehended the killing of the governor before they were
ready to follow the blow, would fruftrate their attempt, and
bring matters to a crifis before they were prepared; but tyrants frequently haften their own doom by their own meafures.

The oppreffive governors were poffeffed of three caftles, and unlefs thefe were reduced, the oppreffion muft become every day more
intolerable: One of the confederates had an amorous connexion
with a fervant-maid in the caftle of Rozberg; fhe, as ufual, fur-
nifhed him with means of entering, and he introduced twenty of
his friends, who feized the caftle and the governor without difficulty.
The caftle at Sarnen was taken by another ftratagem: It was cu-
ftomary on new year's day to bring prefents to the governor; twenty
confederates accordingly appeared at the caftle gates early in the
morning, and made the governor the ufual compliments, armed with
nothing but long ftaves; the governor was juft agoing to mafs, and
as he faw them without arms, ordered them to carry their gifts into the caftle. They had no fooner entered, but they fixed irons
which they had concealed to their fticks, made prifoners of the garrifon,
and the caftle was demolifhed. The governors betook themfelves to
flight, and nobody offered to purfue them. Thus in one day all the
ftrong holds were taken and deftroyed, and the next day the three
cantons folemnly fwore to each other for the fpace of ten years:
This fmall beginning laid the foundation of the republic of Swifferland, which has maintained its freedom and independency until this
time, and nearly furvived the liberty of moft ftates of Europe.

The emperor Albert had now obtained his wifh, viz. a pretext
to reduce the cantons by open war, under pretence of rebellion. He
immediately repaired to Baden, *ftopt all commerce with thefe three
cantons, and ordered his vaffals to declare war againft them*; but while
he meditated war againft an oppreffed people, he was himfelf mur-
dered by his nephew, whofe inheritance he unjuftly detained from
him; his murderer hoped to find a place of retreat among thefe cantons, but the Swifs, zealous for their liberty, were incapable to fecure it by giving an afylum unto criminals; his widow was fo bent
upon avenging the death of her hufband, that fhe took no meafures
againft the Swifs, who had refifted the oppreffions of their tyrannical governors.

Leopold, the fon of Albert, when he came of age, determined to
make war againft the three cantons, and collected an army of 20,000
men for that purpofe; his plan was to attack the confederates the
15th of November, 1311, at a place called Morgarden, fituate between a lake and a mountain. In expectation that the inhabitants

of Underwalden would come to the affistance of the confederates, the Count of Strafberg and the city of Lucern were to invade the cantons at the fame time and at two different places. At dinner he afked the opinion of his jefter, who replied, " All advife how to en-" ter into the country, it feems to me neceffary to confider how to " come out again." His advife was defpifed, but verified by the event. A brave and virtuous people may be attacked, but wo to tyrants that cannot retreat.

The plan was exactly followed ; Leopold made a falfe attack at Arth, and perhaps the confederates would have placed all their little force there, if they had not received an information to " beware at Morgarden." To that place the cantons Ury and Underwalden fent 700 men, and the canton Swifs an equal number, who were pofted on a mountain called the Saddle. On the day appointed the duke of Auftria advanced at the head of his cavalry, his troops marched in great confidence, *"fure to obtain an eafy victory upon peafants, badly armed, and without military difcipline:"* Accordingly they proudly preffed into a defile, when they were ftopt by 50 men, who had been banifhed the cantons for crimes, and whom, notwithftanding their requeft, the confederates would not think worthy to fight for liberty, even upon this preffing occafion. Thefe men, however, by generoufly expofing themfelves for their country, hoped to deferve the pardon of former crimes, they pofted themfelves on a very fteep hill, above a narrow path, where the Auftrian army could not march above two men a-breaft ; they fuffered them very quietly to advance, but when a confiderable number were now engaged in thefe narrow roads, they fent fuch a fhower of ftones and rolled large pieces of timber among the Auftrian cavalry, that they were foon put in confufion ; which the Swifs no fooner perceived, than they fell upon them with fuch fury, that they were obliged to retreat towards the plain ; to gain ground to form the order of battle, the infantry opened their ranks, to let the cavalry pafs ; at this moment the confederates broke in upon them, and ftanding on rifing ground, their halbards did moft dreadful execution. A cotemporary author faith, it was not a fight but a maffacre. The prince loft near 1500 of his horfe, the lofs of the infantry could not be afcertained, but 52 men from Zuric, then in the intereft of Auftria, were all found flain in a heap ; the lofs of the confederates was incredibly trifling: Meanwhile the count of Strafberg, with 4000 men had alfo invaded Underwalden, who fend to their friends at Morgarden, and 400 of the victorious Swifs inftantly fled to their relief; they came up with a body of their own people, with whom they attacked the count, who feeing colours among them that had been at Morgarden, judged his mafter was defeated, and fo fled. The Swifs killed about 300 of his men in the retreat. After this battle gained, the three cantons en-

tered

tered into a perpetual alliance, which no power has since been able to break, and which heaven has remarkably preserved.

One of the next greatest battle the Swifs fought in defence of their liberty, was in the year 1386. Leopold, duke of Austria, personally repaired to Swifferland, in order to carry on the war with greater vigour. The duke had resolved to lay siege to Sempach; the confederates had intelligence of it, and both opposite armies arrived before this little town the very same day. The Austrian advanced guard, confisting of about 1400 men, committed all manner of violence on their territory: One of their officers mounted a cart loaded with halters, and threatened to hang all the inhabitants before funset. The Austrians insulted the Swifs, it being in the time of haymaking, they came so near the walls to speak with them, and defired they would send dinner and wages to their mowers. The Swifs replied, it was not the custom of the Swifs to pay wages till they were earned, and that they would prepare a dinner for them, that many spoons should drop out of their hands. The duke's army consisted of about 4000 picked men, and among them many princes and noblemen, armed from head to foot. The confederates were about 1300 men, badly armed, and all on foot; they had no arms but halbards, and fastened pieces of wood on their arms, to fend off and break the blows of the enemies; their order of battle was very close, and represented an angle, one soldier was followed by two, two by four, and so on; in this order this handful of men courageously advanced against the enemy. Before they begun the engagement, as was usual with them, they fell down to prayers, which made the duke's jester say, " Leopold, my countrymen (for he was a Swifs) " have all lift up their hands, and sworn to almighty GOD, " to kill thee." An Austrian officer, observing their undaunted countenance, advised to delay the battle till next day, but a nobleman declared, " He would deliver that handful of boors before supper into " the hands of the duke roasted or boiled, as he should best like " them." The nobility was so eager to engage, that they dismounted, gave their horses into the care of their servants, and would not suffer any but noblemen to share in the honour of the day. It happened that a young nobleman, in cutting off the long point of his shoe (as all the rest did) wounded his toe, which made him cry, whereupon the nobility ordered him out of the rank, as unworthy to fight. His brethren were all slain, and his life was saved. The battle begun, the superior power of the Austrians in men and arms soon appeared, 60 confederates were killed before they could make the least impression on their enemy; in this distress a brave knight of the family of Winkelried resolved to sacrifice his life for his country, he accordingly advanced boldly, and with his arms grasped and bent

down

down as many of their long pikes as he could hold, the others preffed after him with irrefiftable fury, broke in with their halbards upon the Auftrians, and made dreadful havock.

It is faid, that before the engagement they proclaimed that every man that thought himfelf infufficient to encounter ten Auftrians, might withdraw, and that about 300 withdrew accordingly ; but when thefe faw the Auftrians order of battle broke, they haftened to affift their brethren, and the nobility loft courage, gave way to the Swifs, and many of them, from the heat of the day and feverity of the engagement, were fuffocated by the weight of their own armour. The duke was feveral times entreated to withdraw, but feeing his banner in danger, he generoufly advanced to refcue it, but fell in the attempt. When the fervants, who had been ordered in the rear with the horfes, faw the defeat of their mafters, they mounted their mafters horfes, aud left their mafters to fhift for themfelves. It is fuppofed the lofs of the Auftrians amounted to 2000. including 667 of the nobility, and among them 350 with crowned cafkets. The Swifs loft about 200, who were all carried to their refpective homes. The third day they permitted the enemy to carry off their dead, among whom the duke was the principal; he was carried of the field of battle in a great box (ftill extant), which, 'tis faid, had been full of halters, to hang the confederates. The Swifs, in hopes of obtaining peace, were fparing of the blood of the Auftrians, and did not purfue them in their retreat; they had reafon to repent their lenity, but the continuance of the war ferved only to increafe the victories and fame of the Swifs confederates. The fons of the defeated Leopold made great preparation for war, and many imperial cities joined with them againft the Swifs ; a truce was indeed concluded, which the Auftrians badly kept, and by furprize and fecret intelligence made themfelves mafters of Wefen, the poffeffion of which laid the whole canton of Glaris open to their ravages. The Swifs confederates advifed that canton to get the beft terms poffible, but thofe propofed by the Auftrians were fo exceffive fevere, that that treaty came to nothing. The Auftrians propofed themfelves to invade that country with about 8000 men ; the inhabitants had caft up an entrenchment, which was guarded by about 350 men ; when the Auftrians advanced, thefe finding themfelves to weak to refift, retreated to a rifing ground, the Auftrians penetrated into the country, and burned the village of Nafels, and then attacked the abovementioned handful of inhabitants, who received them with a fhower of ftones ; the Auftrians having retreated a little to put themfelves under cover, the Swifs feized the favourable moment, and fell upon them with fuch fury, that after an engagement of five hours, they were forced to fly. The Swifs purfued and came up with them at

a bridge,

a bridge, where about 700 Swifs had gathered; the Auftrians, in their confufion not aware that the bridge was broke, preffed on, and numbers were drowned. The lofs of the Auftrians was computed at 2000, while that of the Swifs did not exceed 55 men.

The dukes of Auftria again confented to a truce, by which the Swifs were to remain in poffeffion of all their conquefts; this truce in 1314 was renewed for twenty, and in 1412 for fifty years longer. The Swifs made ufe of thefe times of tranquillity to give ʼtability and perfection to their military difciplines. In 1393 they ag... ʼ upon the following regulations among themfelves: 1. No church nor chapel to be attacked, unlefs it is made ufe of as an afylum to the enemy. 2. No woman to be violated or infulted. 3. *Every Swifs engageth to facrifice his fubftance and life for his country.* 4. No Swifs to forfake his poft, even tho' wounded. 5. Forbids to pillage without leave of the commander, and orders the fpoils to be equally divided. 7. All that fend provifions to the Swifs fhall be protected. 8. No canton to make war without the confent of the reft. 9. No Swifs to take away any thing by violence from another, neither in time of war nor peace.

The Swifs carried their military difcipline to fuch perfection, that Machiavel pretends no nations ever exceeded them in that refpect, except the Romans.

On the whole then we may conceive the rife and progrefs of liberty in Swifferland thus: 1. They had fome rights and liberties granted them by emperors, which do not appear very confiderable. 2. The emperors of the houfe of Auftria endeavoured to feparate them from the Roman empire, and bring them in fubjection to the then rifing houfe of Auftria. 3. Againft this the Swifs remonftrated, petitioned and pleaded their charters. 4. Governors were fent among them, who were to, and did, opprefs them, in order to drive them to fome act of defpair, which their enemies intended to term rebellion, and under pretence of it reduce them by force of arms. This, 5. at length produced confederacies, firft only of three men, by degrees of three fmall countries, which encreafed gradually to *thirteen* cantons, befides fome confederates. 6. To fubdue them, a ftop was firft put to their trade, and afterwards they were attacked by force. 7. When attacked, they defended themfelves with incredible bravery, and under every poffible difadvantage refifted every attack. and at laft obliged their enemies not only to defift, but to declare them a free ftate; and furrounded by Auftria, France and Savoy they have continued free and brave ever fince, and may they do fo to the end of time.

The following Tracts are to be had at the Printer:

THE Christian's Hope in Death, exemplified in the last Hours of several pious Persons. 3f.

A Sermon on the Repeal of the Stamp-Act. 6d.

A funeral Sermon for the Rev. Mr. Whitefield. 6d.

Pious Advice of an affectionate Father. 3d.

A Sermon on Faith, with an Appendix in Vindication of the Rev. Mr. Harvey. 1f.

A Letter to the Rev. Mr. Frink, on Fees demanded of Dissenters. 3d.

Thoughts when the day of Judgment may be expected. 9d.

Also to be had:

Great-Britain's Right to tax the Colonies, placed in the clearest Light, by a Swifs. 1f.